To Olga

HAUNT ELY

We hope you enjoy the stories!

Margaret Haynes & Vivienne Doughty

Margaret Haynes
22. XI '08.

The Blue Hand Press

To Emily and Mark

First published in 1996 by S.B. Publications.

Reprinted 1997 and 1999

This reissued edition published in 2003 by The Blue Hand Press, Dove Cottage, 7 Silver Street, Ely, Cambs.

Copyright 2003 Margaret Haynes and Vivienne Doughty

All rights reserved
No part of this publication may be reproduced, stored in a retrieval system, or transmitted in any form or by any means (electronic, mechanical, photocopying, recording or otherwise) without the prior permission of the authors and publishers.

ISBN 0-9545886-0-6

Typeset, printed and bound by Franklyn,
Gorebrook Mill, Pink Bank Lane, Longsight, Manchester, M12 5GH

Contents

Acknowledgements 4
Introduction 5
Map of the Isle of Ely and surrounding islands of the Fens before drainage 7
City of Ely Street Map 8
Plan of The Monastic Buildings in the College at Ely 10

1   The Blue Hands of Saint Etheldreda 12
2   Staffordshire Bull Terriers, Black Shuck and some Furry Phantoms 18
3   Benedictine Monks and other Mysteries 23
4   Elizabeth Goudge and her Firmary Lane Ghosts 28
5   More Monks, a Serving Wench and some Spooky Footprints 35
6   The Commuting Ghosts of Silver Street Cottages 40
7   The Cromwells, a Fenland Legend and some Galloping Hooves 45
8   Ely Tourist Information Centre, Soldiers, an Actress and more Galloping Hooves .. 51
9   A Sergeant Major, a Militia Family, a Nurse and more Monks 57
10 The Bodysnatchers 60
11 Waterside Wraiths 63
12 Witchford's Wartime Secrets 66

About the Authors 71
Bibliography 72

Front Cover
Ely Cathedral's West End and the Cannon on the Green.
Back Cover
Ely Cathedral's Octagon replaced an earlier Norman tower that collapsed one dark February night in 1322.
Title Page
Ely Deanery from Oyster Lane, with the Cathedral in the background (note the open window of Elizabeth Goudge's attic bedroom).

Acknowledgements

The authors are indebted to the following people and organisations.

Arundel Castle Trustees Ltd., Barry Aldridge, Pamela Blakeman, Reg and Anita Brown, Mrs P Butler, Barbara Denisi, Barbara and Tim Eaton, Jean Eames, Barbara and Tony Gipp, Malcolm Graham, Bill Green, Joan Griffin, Very Rev Dr Michael Higgins, Tom Jackson, Chris Jakes, Bunty Jones, Peter J.Lee, Susan Lee, Paul Loose, Chris and Peter Kerswell, Kate Marshall, Connie May, Canon Neil Munt, Liz Nardone, Les Oakey, Jo and Andrew Odell-Rouke, Gill Peak, Graham Peters, Christine Pownell, Tony Ransome, Anabelle Reddick, Rosie Shipley, Mallyan Thompson, Oliver Cromwell's House Staff, Chris Wall, Richard Whitehand, and many others who wish to remain anonymous.

All photographs are by Vivienne Doughty, unless stated otherwise.

Introduction

After taking a spectacular ghost tour of York in 1985, Ely Blue Badge Tourist Guide, Margaret Haynes, was inspired to develop her own local tour from material she had already collected. Any place with an inhabited past is bound to have ghosts. The Isle of Ely's history is equally as long and fascinating as that of York, and the surrounding, flat, black Fenland reputedly the most haunted area of Britain.

A former Dean of Ely observed that 'Any good tour operator will tell you ghosts are good for business', and in this case he was right. Margaret's tours began the following year and were immediately popular, especially among local people, who began to divulge their own curious experiences. Many an unwilling ghost-spotter who had preferred to keep quiet for years, fearing ridicule, now confided in Margaret's sympathetic ear.

No one expects to experience unearthly events, and those who do, often hesitate to trust their own eyes. But seeing is believing, and even the most reluctant witness finds it difficult not to tell at least one person. Colleagues disbelieve. Friends are sceptical. A much repeated old joke suggests that overindulgence in strong brew at one of the city's many pubs, is the trigger for such sightings - but how many transparent, hooded monks have you seen after a night on the tiles? Those who encounter ghosts - firemen, nurses, teachers, plumbers, security guards, vicars' wives, writers - are as sober as you and me.

Even that most factual of creatures - the aforementioned Dean - admits that 'at the bottom of these stories there is a grain of truth', though he prefers to think 'profit motive is at the heart of many stories.' It is true that ghost books sell well, which is perhaps why a local bookseller urged Margaret to write one. Customers to her shop were often disappointed to find no literature on Ely's alternative population, though plenty of other ghost books lined the shelves. Margaret herself owned a large collection, yet had never come across a single mention of Ely.

Time was her problem. She had been inundated with so many intriguing new stories to add to her existing ones, that the resulting material would no longer fit into an hour long tour. Second and third tours had to be developed for those enthusiastic groups who returned each year for more. Her fame spread throughout East Anglia, and she began to appear on local radio and television. With an increasingly busy schedule of ghost tours - as well as history tours, drama tours and evening talks - the stories remained inside her head.

She needed a ghost writer and approached me. We were both Ely Blue Badge Tourist Guides with a shared passion for local history. Margaret's second interest was ghosts. Mine was writing. It seemed the perfect combination. She told the stories and I wrote them down. We checked with our local sources before including their names in the book, and those who preferred to remain anonymous were given false names. For every person who is happy to share an unexplained experience, another is not.

Most of our ghosts are anonymous, but it can be difficult not to jump to conclusions. Hooded monks are obviously Benedictines from the great medieval monastery that put Ely on the map. A brooding male presence in the only home inhabited by Oliver Cromwell that he would recognise were he to return (which he does), must be the great man himself; the homely woman who flits along corridors with a bunch of keys at her waist is bound to be Mrs Cromwell. A shady character seen lurking in St Mary's churchyard with a spade, is surely one of the 19th century body snatchers who earned a good living from that much frequented haunt.

There are no headless horsemen, knights in clanking armour or lamenting ladies roaming cloisters by moonlight and wringing their hands. The fact is that real ghosts (if you will excuse the oxymoron) are just as likely to be spotted strolling down Ely High Street on a sunny summer afternoon as flitting around ruins at midnight in the dead of winter. Occasionally we have been tempted to put two and two together and make five. Put it down to artistic license. Ghosts do not exist in a vacuum, and we have fitted ours snugly into local history. What follows is an alternative history of Ely, related through the activities of its ghost population.

Vivienne Doughty, November 2003

Map of the Isle of Ely and surrounding islands of the Fens before drainage.

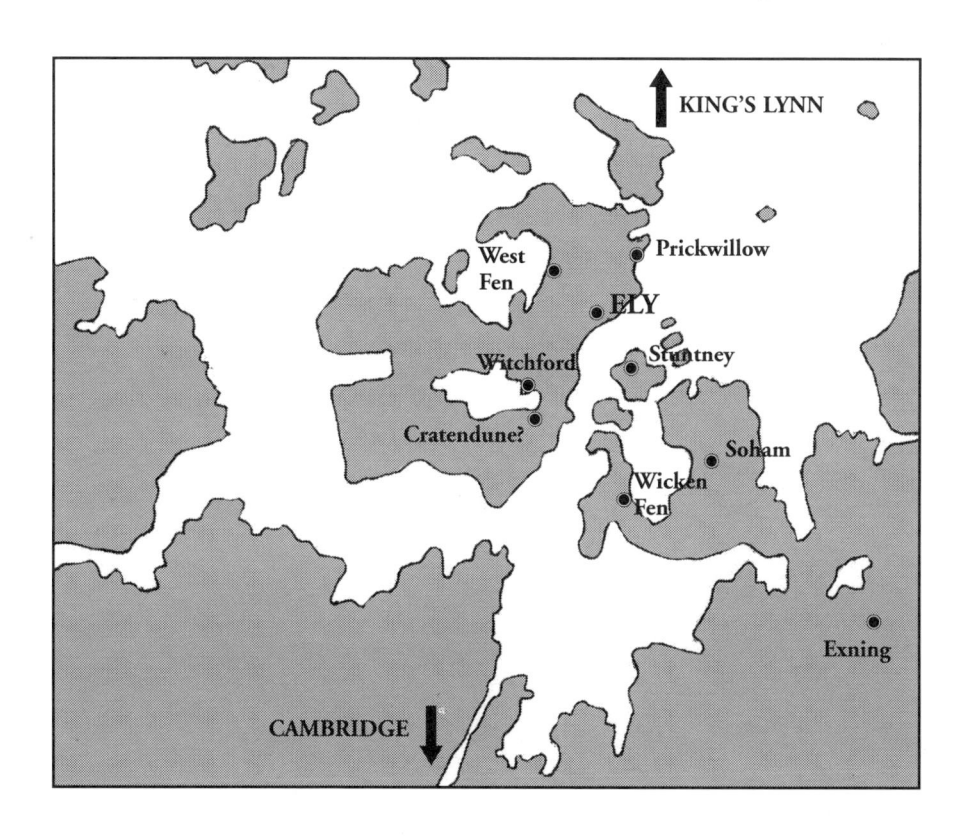

8

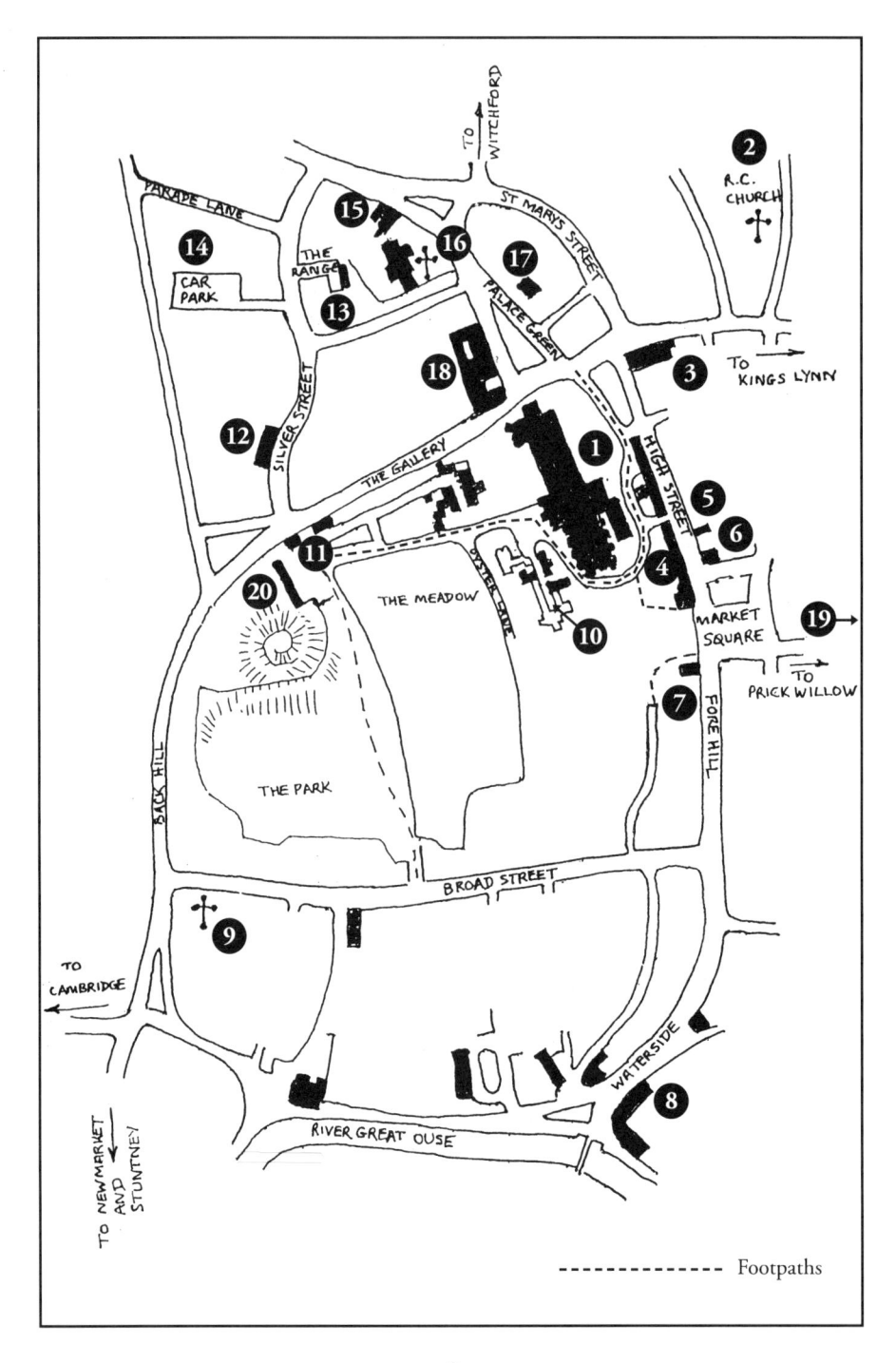

City of Ely Street Map

Showing some of the sites referred to in the book

1. The Cathedral
2. St Etheldreda's RC Church
3. The Lamb Hotel
4. The North Range
5. Pizza Express (formerly Peck's the Ironmongers)
6. Peter Dominic (formerly The Dolphin public house)
7. Johnsons the Cleaners (formerly The Monks' Gate)
8. Waterside Antiques
9. St Peter's Church
10. Firmary Lane
11. The Porta
12. Silver Street Cottages
13. Former Militia Hospital
14. Cathedral car park (formerly the Militia Parade Ground)
15. Oliver Cromwell's House, Ely Tourist Information Centre
16. St Mary's Church
17. The Chantry
18. The Bishop's Palace
19. To The Highflyer public house
20. The King's School dining room and kitchens (formerly monastery stables and barns)

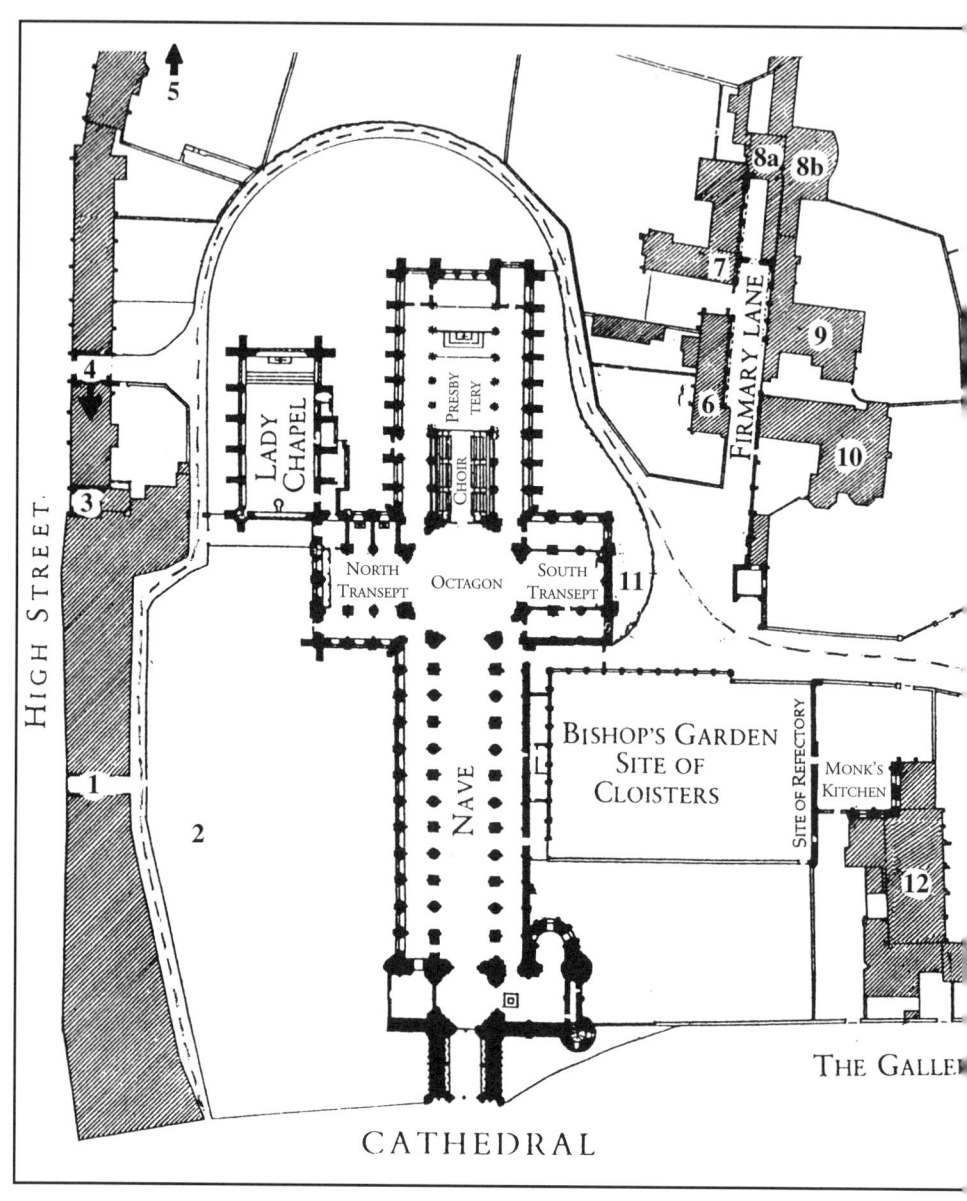

1 The Steeple Gate
2 St Cross Green
3 The Goldsmith's Tower
4 The Sacrist's Gate,
5 Johnson the Cleaners (site of the Monks' Gate)
6 Powcher's Hall
7 The Choir House (also known as Walsingham House and The Painted Chamber)
8a The Chapter Office & part of the Deanery

Plan of The Monastic Buildings in the College at Ely

By Courtesy of Ely Cathedral

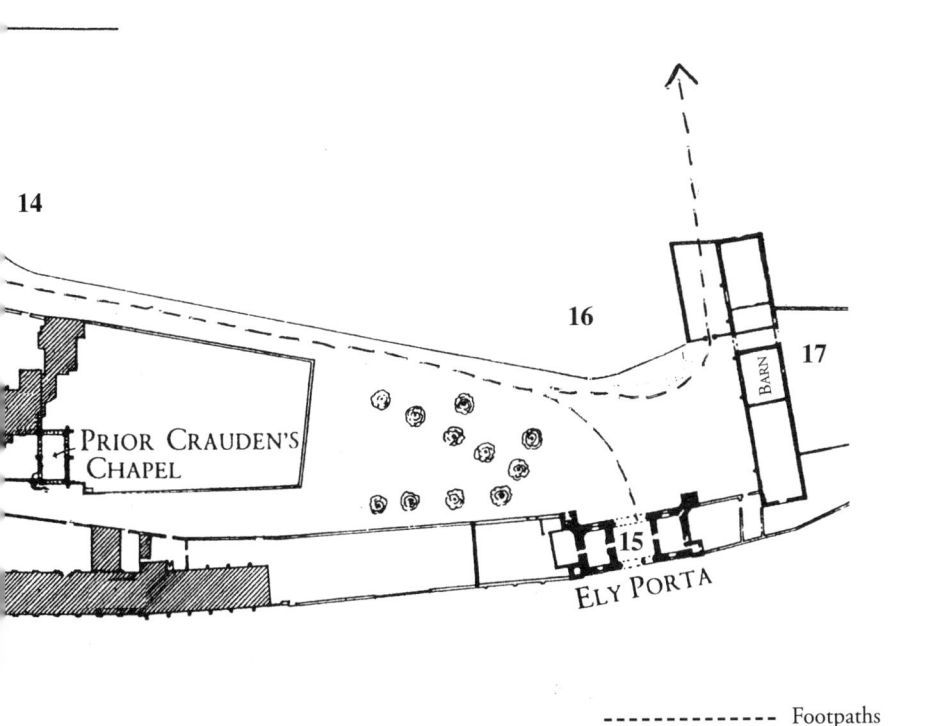

PRIOR CRAUDEN'S CHAPEL

BARN

ELY PORTA

------------- Footpaths

8b The Deanery's Victorian extension
9   The Black Hostelry
10 Canonry House
11 Site of the Slype
12 Bishop's House
13 Priory House
14 The Dean's Meadow
15 The Porta
16 The Park
17 The Monastery Stables (now King's School dining room and kitchens)

1 The Blue Hands of Saint Etheldreda

St Etheldreda's hands haunt the history of the city she founded on the Isle of Ely in 672 AD. Her ghostly hand glides up the back staircase banister of Priory House, a junior boys' boarding-house at one of England's oldest public schools. The King's School, where Edward the Confessor studied as a boy, was founded in 970 AD and refounded after the Reformation in 1541, by Henry VIII. The saint's physical hand resides in Ely too, enshrined inside a bell-shaped reliquary in a niche above the font of St Etheldreda's Catholic Church in Egremont Street. But who was Etheldreda and why are her hands linked with Ely?

The Isle of Ely - or Eel Island - was the largest of several islands that lay marooned for centuries among the fens of East Anglia. The low-lying pockets of land, none rising more than a few feet above the surrounding swamp, were home to a squat, dark haired, round skulled race, who were rumoured to possess yellow-bellies and webbed feet - like frogs. They lived by their own laws in wattle and daub huts, slept on beds of dried reeds with bulrushes for pillows, and cooked over smoky fires of dried peat. Lives were short in the damp, fever-ridden marshes, though the diet was healthy enough - a mixture of fish, fowl and iron-rich water plants, hunted and gathered along precarious pathways that crossed the water-logged land.

Such a remote, inhospitable, place was the perfect setting for a religious community, and in the early 7th century, as Christianity was beginning to scratch the surface of Britain, the princess who would begin such an establishment, was born. She was one of the four remarkable daughters of King Anna and Queen Hereswitha of the East Angles, early converts to the new religion. The princesses, Ethelburga, Sexburga, Withburga and Etheldreda, soon followed their parents' lead. They wished to serve God as nuns but their father insisted they serve him first, and found husbands for them among neighbouring rulers whose lands bordered his court at Exning, the old East Anglian capital, not far from present day Newmarket.

Princess Etheldreda was betrothed to Tondbert, Prince of the Fens, on her own condition that she remain chaste. The prince died of fen-ague (a shivering disease carried by mosquitoes) a couple of years after the nuptials - leaving the Isle of Ely to his wife. The wealthy, young virgin-widow moved to her new estate and started planning a religious foundation. Yet hardly had she begun, when a second, younger, healthier bridegroom was produced for her.

The twenty eight year old princess was obliged to leave her island refuge and travel north to York for a marriage with the thirteen year old Prince Egfrith of Northumbria. Such an ill-matched pair were never destined to be happy, and after a few years of wedded incompatibility in his cold, northern land, the princess persuaded her husband to let her enter a convent at Coldingham, in the Scottish borders and take her vows. But when Egrith became king, he needed an heir and set off to collect his mature wife by force.

The unwilling Queen Ethedreda, her virginity still intact, fled down the east coast with her servants, on the long journey back to Ely, pursued by her husband and his men. As he closed in on his quarry at St Ebbs Head, there was 'a sudden and unusual inundation of water from the sea, which surrounded the hill' and marooned the king's party for several days. He interpreted this as a warning from Heaven, and gave up the chase. The fugitive queen crossed the River Humber about ten miles west of Hull, and founded a church in thanksgiving. When she stuck her wooden staff into the ground, it took root and grew into a tree.

St Ethedreda and her flowering staff are depicted on a brick wall at Ely's Tesco Supermarket, Angel Drove.

Back on her island, Etheldreda established a double monastery for monks and nuns, not far from the existing Saxon settlement of Cratendune, and spent her last few years as abbess, dying in 679 of a tumour on her throat, which she believed was a punishment for vanity. (She had been partial to showy necklaces in her youth.) Her body lay in the nuns' graveyard for sixteen years, until her sister Sexburga - second abbess and widow of the king of Kent - decided to move it to a more prestigious tomb inside the abbey-church. When the coffin was opened, the body was found to be undecayed. The tumour was gone, and a spring of pure water bubbled from the empty grave.

The queen and abbess was pronounced a saint. Her smart, new tomb was revered, as were the later ones of Abbess Sexburga, and her daughter, Ermenilda (widow of Wulfere, king of Mercia), who had followed as third abbess. The monastery was destroyed in 870 by marauding Vikings, but re-established a hundred years later by Benedictine monks, who moved the bodies of the three holy women into the next church. When this building was replaced more than a hundred years later by William the Conqueror's great Norman cathedral, the remains were moved again, as soon as the new choir was ready.

Holy bones were a magnet to medieval pilgrims, who enjoyed travelling around the country visiting shrines with like-minded companions. These very first tourists stayed in the very first hotels - residential hostels provided by religious houses who wanted their business. Hostels identified themselves with painted signs, as few people were able to read. Ely's hostel was known by the sign of the *Agnus Dei* or *Lamb of God*, one of the earliest inn signs, that was later shortened to *The Lamb*. Built conveniently close to the monastery, it would later develop into the Lamb Inn - and long outlast the tombs that caused it to be built.

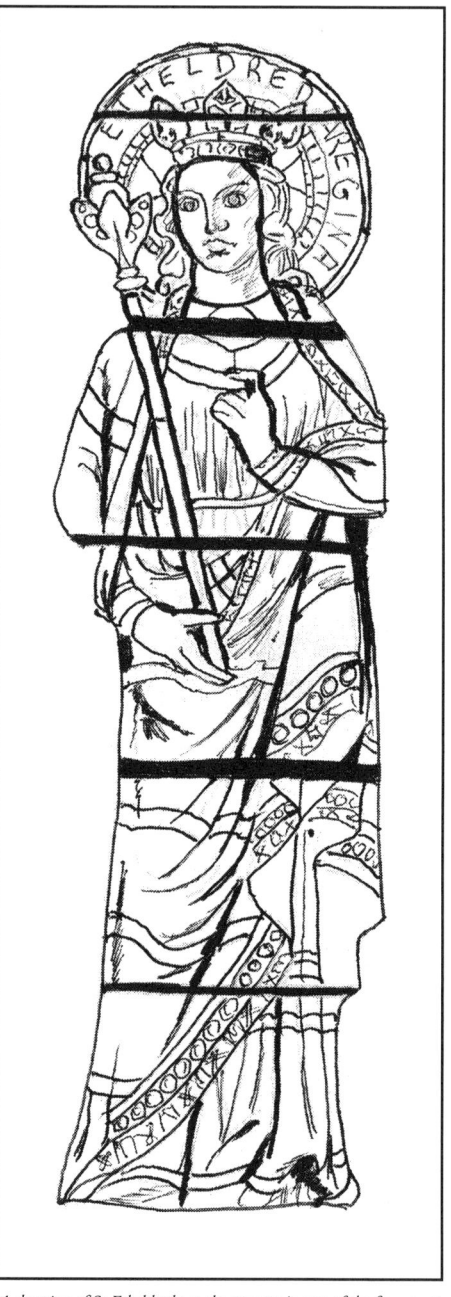

A drawing of St Etheldreda as she appears in one of the four great stained glass windows made by William Wailes in the 1860s for the Octagon.

But while the Middle Ages lasted, the shrines of the three royal abbesses - princesses by birth, queens by marriage and saints by reputation - proved such a popular attraction that the cathedral was extended by three bays at the east end to accommodate more pilgrims, and the peripatetic saints moved for the last time. The sick and weary flocked to the shrines, and left generous gifts if they were restored to health, as they often were. Faith and a change of scenery can work miracles.

All this munificence ended in 1539 when Henry VIII broke with the Roman Catholic Church and made himself head of a reformed Protestant church that would not tolerate such 'childish superstitions'. The king wanted no foreign interference in his affairs. The Pope's name was removed from the prayer book and all monastic land confiscated and given to Henry's supporters.

Ely's Bishop Goodrich obliged his earthly boss, ordering that all images, relics and shrines be 'so totally demolished and obliterated that no remains or memory be found of them.' But he kept his options open, balancing the whims of a present anti-Catholic king against the future whims of a possible, succeeding, pro-Catholic one. The crafty cleric supervised the decapitation of more than three hundred statues (off with their heads rather than his own), the smashing of medieval stained glass windows and the destruction of the lucrative shrines. But he avoided the demolition of monastic buildings - which is why so many survive in Ely when most other English monasteries are crumbling ruins.

How did the monks react when the Bishop's henchmen obliterated their history, destroyed their livelihood, smashed their sacred shrines and dumped the bodies of their beloved saints? They rescued bits and pieces that could be hidden among their robes. It would not have been possible to smuggle an entire saint's body past the watchful soldiers - though they were Catholic too and some may have looked the other way - but detached hands and feet could be stuffed inside habits, popped into hoods or hidden up sleeves. In those superstitious times, saintly parts were believed to possess supernatural powers and were much valued by persecuted Catholics, obliged to practice their religion secretly. In monasteries across England, brave brothers salvaged saintly souvenirs and shoved them inside chimney pots, behind panelling and underneath floorboards. Most of the items were lost when their rescuers died, but some have resurfaced from time to time.

Saint Ethedreda's left hand turned up in 1810 on the Duke of Norfolk's Arundel Estate, in Sussex. The relic is thought to have been discovered by the 11th Duke, Charles Howard (1746-1815), known affectionately as the 'Drunken Duke', after he was observed riding a barrel of beer during an election campaign. His more serious hobby was architecture. The Duke redesigned and reconstructed the castle in 1815, and was doing a spot of DIY on his decaying estate buildings, when a reliquary containing the saint's hand, came to light behind the demolished wall of a priest's hole, in an estate farmhouse.

The Dukes of Norfolk had been heads of the Roman Catholic Church in England since the Reformation - which was presumably why the saintly souvenir ended up there

- but the 11th Duke, had converted to Anglicanism, and gave the hand away to his estate agent, Mr Harting, who was a fervent Catholic. By the time the Catholic 12th Duke inherited the title, the agent's son had handed the relic on to his daughter, Sister Aquinas, a nun at St Dominic's Priory in Stone, Staffordshire. In a letter to his daughter, Mr Harting junior wrote: 'The relic is fitted on a silver spike rising from a circular plate of silver on which are inscribed the words 'Manus Scae Etheldreda 679', and (is) enclosed in a bell-shaped ivory case on an ebony stand with ivory ball supports.'

It changed hands again in 1953 when St Dominic's chauffeur, Mary Pritchard, gave it to her brother, Father Guy Pritchard, for the Golden Jubilee celebrations of the founding of St Etheldreda's Catholic Church in Ely, where he was parish priest. Father Pritchard lived next door in the presbytery with a mischievous poltergeist who opened drawers, banged doors and threw pans around in the middle of the night, but as soon as St Etheldreda's hand arrived, the spirit left.

The thirteen hundred year old hand was blueish-white when Sunday school teacher, Mallyan Thompson, saw it during the following weekend's festivities, but exposure has since turned it brown. The ghostly hand was blue too - appropriately a luminous royal blue - when three mesmerised King's School boys watched it gliding up the curved banister of Priory House's back staircase towards their tower bedroom, as they shivered beneath duvets on a warm summer night in 1995.

Priory House tower, where the ghostly blue hand of St Etheldreda glides up the back staircase banister towards the top bedroom.

2 Staffordshire Bull Terriers, Black Shuck and some Furry Phantoms

During the superstitious times of the Middle Ages, sinners' hands were believed to possess supernatural powers too and were easier to obtain than those of saints as there were more of them about. Hands were cut from executed thieves and murderers as they dangled still warm from the gallows, by fellow thieves and murderers who had not yet been caught. These ghoulish lucky charms were preserved by secret recipe and shaped into quirky candleholders to light the homes of chosen victims on moonless nights. The grisly amulets were reputed to contain magic powers that kept tenants asleep while intruders stripped their place bare - and usually worked - for should any householder awake to such a sight, his eyes would close again pretty quickly.

The 11th century local hero of Charles Kingsley's 1866 historical novel, 'Hereward the Wake', spies a 'Hand of Glory' illuminating the corner of a fenland hovel on the edge of Ely, site of the Saxons' Last Stand in 1077 against the hated Norman invaders. In the story, Hereward disguises himself as a potter and sets out to find the enemy camp: '. . . stuck against the wall, was something which chilled Hereward's blood a little - a dried human hand, which he knew must have been stolen off the gallows, gripping in its fleshless fingers a candle, which he knew was made of human fat. That candle, he knew, duly lighted and carried, would enable the witch to walk unseen into any house on earth, yea, through the court of King William himself, while it drowned all men in preternatural slumber.'

In reality, Hereward and the remnants of the raggle-taggle, Anglo-Saxon army had retreated into Ely's abbey, where the tombs of the three saintly queens still lay in splendour before the altar. William the Conqueror had subdued the south of England, but needed to overcome this last pocket of resistance to make his conquest complete. The Normans camped beyond the marshes at Cambridge, while they searched for an existing secret causeway into the isle and attempted to construct new ones of their own.

Nearly 800 years later, Victorian writers transformed the unruly East Anglian outlaw - himself a descendant of earlier Danish invaders - into a Fenland version of Robin Hood, substituting Robin's dark, shorn hair and neat goatee for Hereward's blonde, bobbed haircut and bird-nest beard. Guerrilla fighters replaced merry men.

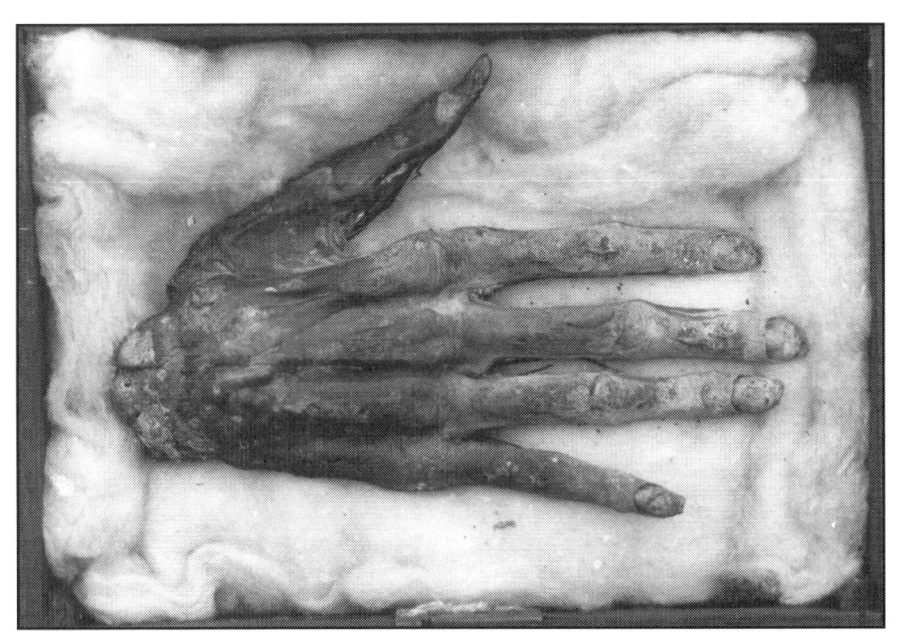

'The Hand of Glory' is on display at Whitby Museum. Amputated hands were believed to have supernatural powers. This one was found in the early 1900s, hidden behind bricks, above the door lintel of a cottage in Danby, North Yorkshire, and may have been used as late as 1820. Photograph courtesy of Whitby Museum.

Lincoln-green became fenland-brown, and Little John was supplanted by Hereward's best friend - his trusty hound.

But is 'hound' an apt description? When Cambridge University archaeologists discovered carefully laid out dogs' graves during the 1999 excavation of an extensive Saxon settlement to the west of Ely, they unearthed the bones of small stocky dogs with powerful jaws - similar to Staffordshire Bull Terriers. 'There is a definite element of caring that has gone into the way the dogs have been buried', said Roddy Regan of the university team. 'My guess is they were sheep dogs or herding dogs.'

The Saxon freedom-fighters were probably betrayed by their own side. Abbot Thurstan disliked the use of his precious abbey as a soldiers' barracks, and in any case, realised the futility of further resistance. His monks are though to have guided the enemy into the isle, hoping to spare the rich monastery. But the Normans took everything. They replaced the Saxon Thurstan with a Norman abbot and the Saxon abbey with a Norman cathedral, but kept the lucrative shrines, moving them to a penultimate position in front of the new high altar.

Hereward vanished into history but perhaps his dog still haunts the ancient footpaths that he once trod. A phantom-hound, sometimes known as Black Shuck, crosses the Ely/Cambridge section of the A10 between Braham Farm and the old Witchford aerodrome site around dusk, causing chaos during the early evening rush hour. He takes the track that borders the fen-edge between Angel Drove and

Great Dane: Hereward the Wake, with the fair Torfrida (Fenland's answer to Maid Marion), and his trusty hound. Illustration by Gertrude Demain Hammond for 'The Story of Hereward' by Douglas C. Stedman, 1909. Photograph courtesy of Ely Museum

Wake's Meadow housing site - and a 21st century dog. The twenty acre site along West Fen Road was continually inhabited between the 8th and 15th centuries, and is soon to be inhabited again. In 1999, during a Cambridge University dig, archaeologists found 138,000 animal bones - sheep, pig, cattle, horses and carefully buried dogs. The Saxon archaeology dates to around 1070 and 'exactly fits with Hereward - he would have been here'.

Witchford village, where the soft padding of his feet can be heard not far from the site of the dogs' graves.

Paul Loose had never heard of Black Shuck when he moved into an isolated cottage at Brandon Bank, near Ely in 1996, but as he exercised his dogs on the fen that very first evening, glittering red eyes winked at him from the darkness. The following week, Paul read an account of the phantom- hound in the *Ely Standard*. According to the newspaper, the dog's name derives from the Anglo-Saxon word 'soucca' meaning demon. He bounds along Devil's Dyke, a 6th century bank-and-ditch earthwork that stretches from the Suffolk hills to the fen edge, and along the riverbank at Prickwillow, where young Albert Gipp used to watch him from the window of the tiny cottage he shared with his parents in the 1930s. In the 1960s, Mr and Mrs C. Fuller thought they had run him over, when a big black dog darted in front of their car by the Cherry Tree public house, as they drove along the A142 towards Downfield's Mill in Soham. They stopped and looked underneath, but he was not there. Nor did he appear on the opposite footpath that leads to the National Trust's 800 acre Wicken Fen, where he supposedly 'pads noiselessly along Spinney Bank with his blood red eyes as large as saucers.'

Perhaps these sightings explain the mysterious 'Fen Tiger', the most popular topic of the *Fortean Times* in 1996. Wildlife enthusiast, William Rooker of Impington village (between Ely and Cambridge), caught the shadowy creature on video one morning, while hiding in bushes with his camera, hoping to film turtle doves. Later that week he found himself at the other end of a lens. After appearing in all the national newspapers, he said he would look the other way if he ever saw the creature again.

Other 'sane, adult witnesses' in Cambridge reported a large, black creature lurking near the University Library and St John's College School. Jim Williams, the school's head grounds man (a 'solid, no-nonsense chap'), saw it when he opened the gates at 6.30 am. 'What I saw was not a dog, not a muntjac deer, not a fox,' he said. 'It was a black animal, that's all I know. It just ghosted past me.' When the news spread, headmaster, Kevin Jones, had difficulty keeping 145 excited pupils away from the sports field, but the RSPCA refused to take any action until the creature's physical existence was proved - which has not as yet happened.

Anne Bradford, author of *Midland Ghosts and Hauntings*, says that animal ghosts are usually bad news, but Ely boasts a friendly version of Black Shuck. He appeared to local woman, Connie May, when she visited friends in Cambridge Road, during the early 1950s. She left their house rather late. All the street lights went off at midnight in those days, even on the main road, so she walked quickly beneath the high, thick hedges that grew along the tops of the garden walls. Connie takes up the tale: 'Suddenly a big black dog appeared from nowhere and walked beside me. I'm not keen on dogs, but he was terribly comforting.' The dog accompanied her all the way home to the Victorian house in Chapel Street, where she lived with her family. As she unlocked the door, he settled down beside the gate, but when she turned round, he was gone. Connie never saw him again.

A kitchen had been added to the May's house before they bought it, and a shadowy cat used to sit in the corner where the original door had been. Connie was sure her husband saw the creature too, though he would never admit it. Over time, five children and various solid cats joined and left the household, and still the ghost cat sat in the corner. One evening as she was cooking dinner, her husband opened the back door and then closed it again. 'He said he was letting the cat out, but our cat was in the sitting room with the children.' Connie asked him the colour of the cat and he said it was black. Their own cat was tortoiseshell. 'You've seen the ghost cat the children talk about!' she told him triumphantly. Even visitors would open the back door for the feline phantom - but when a fitted kitchen was installed it vanished for ever.

3 Benedictine Monks and other Mysteries

The enclosed area surrounding Ely cathedral has been known as The College ever since the monastery was dissolved by Henry VIII in 1539, and possesses the largest collection of surviving monastic buildings anywhere in Britain. As they were inhabited for over 600 years by Benedictine monks, it is no surprise that their presence is still felt. All the buildings have been altered, extended and adapted to new uses over the centuries, yet many of their former occupants still recognise and return to their old haunts.

One gregarious old spook attends Evensong in the cathedral, sitting among members of the present congregation in the 14th century choir stalls. Derek Butler, head verger during the 1970s and 80s, used to talk of an old fenman who muttered to himself during service. One evening he asked Derek the name of the clerical gentleman who usually sat beside him and enjoyed a bit of a gossip. When the verger assured the old man that he always sat alone, he became agitated and described the hooded black

Head Verger Derek Butler's stone carved likeness looks down over the College from a pinnacle above the Lady Chapel. Photograph courtesy of Mrs P. Butler

robe and sandals worn by his friendly neighbour. 'He's gone now', he said, 'but when we stopped to talk, he was behind you.'

A more taciturn old soul prefers the peace of the north triforium, former site of Ely's Stained Glass Museum, founded in 1972 to rescue fine glass from derelict churches. Invigilator, Gill Peake glimpsed him in the autumn of 1993, seven years before the museum was transferred to the south triforium. 'It seems funny that for such an important event I never made any record of it in my diary', she pondered. 'At the time it seemed so incredible that I expect I thought I should always remember.'

The museum was situated above the nave's left aisle. Access was through an oak door approached by a spiral staircase in the north transept. The morning visitors had all left, so a movement by the doorway caught Gill's eye as she paused half way along the exhibition area by the Victorian glass, to pick up a dropped entry ticket. 'At first I thought it was a woman in a dark swirling coat and Paddington Bear hat - an extremely solid figure. I thought she'd gone into the alcove to look at the medieval glass.'

Gill approached the alcove intending to ask the woman to pay, but found it empty. The doorway was always in view so it was impossible for anyone to leave without being seen. At this point there was a dramatic drop in temperature. 'Something's wrong here', she thought, and suddenly realised that the visitor was not a woman at all. 'You wally, Gill!' she said to herself. *'It was a Benedictine!* The long, dark coat was his habit and the oddly shaped hat, his cowl. The name "Brother Thomas" popped into my head. I wasn't afraid, though the fine hair on my arms stood on end. The temperature returned to normal and I felt incredible serenity and peace right until I went home and I decided that, yes, I'd seen my second ghost.'

Gill can put a date to the sighting of her first ghost. He was not a monk but retired cathedral cleric, Canon Bawtree, who died in November 1988. She saw him at dusk the following February, ambling out of Oyster Lane on the cathedral's south side, with his arthritic collie - who died the year before - dawdling behind. 'He was walking in the familiar way with his hands behind him, holding the lead.' When she looked again they had gone.

While the museum remained in the north triforium, Gill would sit behind her desk and sense the presence of her soul-mate, and a feeling of serenity would steal over her. 'Brother Thomas and I have something in common. We both love this place and maybe that's why he comes to say hello.' The rest of the museum staff never saw Gill's 'Brother Thomas' and she has not seen him since - but she knows a dog who has.

He was a black and white border collie who attended the cathedral's Wood Green Animal Shelter Pet Service of 2001, postponed until October 20th that year because of the Foot and Mouth epidemic. Gill was sitting six bays down on the left of the nave, next to the collie's owners and their other dog, a Heinz-fifty-seven-variety. The three humans chattered for a while before the service started, and Gill patted the friendly collie, who rolled over to have his tummy rubbed. The service began, as usual, with the congregation singing *All Things Bright and Beautiful*, accompanied, as usual, by much enthusiastic barking and howling. Canon John Inge processed down the aisle followed by the St John's Ambulance representative and his mascot dog.

Gill was tickling the collie behind his ears when he jerked his head away and fixed his eyes on the first floor level of the north triforium. His ears shot up and remained there for the rest of the service. He began to whimper and wag his tail excitedly. She tried to distract him until it dawned on her that he was staring towards the very area where she had seen Brother Thomas. The collie's female owner whispered 'He can see something he likes up there!' but Gill did not reply. Not everyone appreciates ghost stories. At the end of the service, the collie was reluctant to leave and had to be dragged out through the west doorway by his lead. 'Whatever he saw thrilled him to bits, but how strange that he sat next to me!'

Outside the west door, St Cross Green (a former parish graveyard) separates the north side of the cathedral from a footpath that skirts the medieval buildings of the North Range, and winds through the College to Ely Porta - the monastery's Great Gateway. In the mid 14th century, the North Range, workshops and yards were developed by talented sacrist, Alan of Walsingham, to accommodate the scores of skilled craftsmen who flocked to Ely to rebuild the cathedral's central tower, after it collapsed one dark February night in 1322.

On a bright July morning in 2001, two cowled monks strolled along the path as local street cleaner, Richard Whitehand, was emptying the big blue refuse bin behind the Goldsmith's Tower (now used by High Street shop, 'Jumpers'). 'I felt a cold chill,' Richard told an *Ely Standard* reporter later that day, 'and looked up to see two monks in cassocks - one was wearing a brown one and one a black - coming through the gate of the cathedral. I was so scared I dropped everything and froze on the spot. I thought at first someone was mucking about!' The monks drifted across the grass and disappeared into the north transept through the 17th century neo-Norman doorway attributed to Sir Christopher Wren. About half an hour later they reappeared, and returned through the arched gateway by the public toilets, turning right behind the Lady Chapel.

Richard contacted the Very Rev Dr Michael Higgins, who was Dean of Ely

The present Chapter Office and its entrance yard, have been converted from the medieval hospital chapel. The Dean's study, where a former visitors' manager accosted a ghost one day, occupies the roof space of the chancel, with windows facing east and west. The west window looks down Firmary Lane, haunted by at least three ghosts.

between 1991 and 2003. Dr Higgins suggested that he should speak to the apparitions if he ever saw them again - which he did the following week, in the same area but during the afternoon. Following the Dean's advice, he approached the spooky pair and said politely 'Hello, are you alright?' The monks ignored him and continued along the same route as before. When Richard's story was splashed across the front page of the Ely Standard, the Dean decided to add his own pennyworth. In the following week's edition, he used his Viewpoint column 'Dean's Despatch' to comment on the incident, asking 'are people who see ghosts touched themselves or is there truth in their stories?' ('Ghosts or God, where's the difference?' replied N.Smith from the Letter Page the week after that.)

The Dean should be an expert on the subject. He and his wife, Margaret, shared their home of twelve years, The Deanery, with no fewer than three resident ghosts, and their back lane with at least three more. Disappointingly, he claimed that he had personally 'never even seen a shadow disappearing down a corridor'. In his opinion, those who see ghosts 'are not two buttresses short of a Cathedral but are simply drawing attention to themselves. If you are a workman doing monotonous tasks all day then it adds spice to life to say you saw a ghost.' Well he would say that, wouldn't he?

'Monk-y business at the Cathedral' punned the Ely Standard (August 2nd 2001), when Richard Whitehand saw two hooded monks near the Christopher Wren doorway.
Photograph courtesy of the Ely Standard

4 Elizabeth Goudge and her Firmary Lane Ghosts

In her autobiography *The Joy of The Snow*, early 20th century novelist Elizabeth Goudge, who lived in The Deanery as a girl, wrote about the faceless monk that visited her attic bedroom - the same room that would be used towards the end of the century by the Very Rev Dr Michael Higgins and his wife, Margaret.

Elizabeth moved to Ely with her parents when her father, the Reverend Henry Leighton Goudge, was appointed a cathedral canon and principal of the Theological College, now part of the King's School. Their home - not yet revamped as The Deanery - consisted of an 12th century monastic core with 14th and 19th century additions. Strangely, its resident monk did not haunt the oldest part of the house nearest the

The Deanery faces Oyster Lane and looks across the Dean's Meadow to the park. Elizabeth Goudge's former bedroom window is at the top

cathedral, but the Victorian, second floor addition that faces Oyster Lane and looks across the Dean's Meadow to Ely Park. Elizabeth would wake suddenly in the night and see him standing by the bed. 'He was not a frequent visitor. Nor is he now. For I was not alone in seeing that ghost. Subsequent dwellers in the house have seen him too. I do not know how he appeared to them but to me he appeared as a grey-cowled monk with no face. Where his face should have been there was only darkness.'

Eventually the poor girl plucked up courage and told her stern father about the nocturnal visitor. He was not an imaginative man, in common with the building's late 20th century tenant, who was to observe in his weekly *Ely Standard* column : '. . . there is little doubt that a few ghost stories stuck into Miss Goudge's books made them more interesting than they otherwise would have been.' However, the Rev Goudge offered to swop rooms with his daughter for a night so he could investigate the spooky spectre personally before making a decision. Naturally he saw nothing, but did hear lots of noises - mice scuttling, wind howling, windowpanes rattling - and agreed that Elizabeth should have a quieter room. It was no use. Wherever she moved, the faceless fellow followed. 'He was not a pleasant person, not like the angel figure who haunted the next-door house but one.'

This was Canonry House, originally built as a 12th century Cellarer's Hall, but so changed in appearance by a hotchpotch of 14th, 18th and 19th century extensions, that from the outside it is scarcely recognisable as medieval. Only three infilled arches

Canonry House, with Oyster Lane on the right.

incorporated into a side wall betray its Norman origin. Behind the arches lies a 20th century shower-block that might amaze the Cellarer, were he to return. He would have bathed no more than three times a year, whether he needed to or not.

In the early 20th century, the motley pile was home to the Goudge family's neighbours, Canon and Mrs Glazebrook. Their resident ghost was so unusual that they came to the conclusion that perhaps it was not one at all. 'For what ghost stands still to have its portrait painted?' Mrs Glazebrook dabbled in water colours. She enjoyed life drawing and used the female phantom as a model. It was an inspired choice. Her sitter would never wriggle, sneeze, or disappear without warning to put the kettle on. But what must have been the Canon's opinion of his wife's unusual subject? He was probably pleased she had a little hobby to keep her occupied. When the proud artist showed her masterpiece to Mrs Goudge, Elizabeth had a good look too, and observed later that the painting depicted 'a figure in a long robe, resembling a saint in a stained glass window.'

Yet, though the Canonry ghost was bewitching, it frightened some of the Glazebrook's house guests 'for it appeared in the spare room, and guests from the outside world were not acclimatised to the unexplainable as we were who lived always in the shadow of history and legend.' One nervous visitor regretted taking an early night when she caught sight of the figure standing by the wall opposite her bed in the moonlight. She tugged frantically at her bedside bell rope and hid under the covers until the old housemaid answered her call. 'Why, that's nothing to be afraid of,' said the servant, who regarded the ghost as part of the family. 'I can see it in my room too and I call it my angel. When the moonlight leaves the wall it will go.'

The Angel in the Moonlight was a double ghost, appearing larger in the first floor guest room and smaller in the maid's room above, whenever the moon shone through the window onto a certain part of the wall. It seemed to be the reflection of a stained glass window - only there was no such window. The image might have been caused by moonlight revealing the outline of a hidden fresco - only that would not occur in two rooms.

Canonry House later became a boarding-house for King's School girls. Twenty-first century boarders have seen no angels but those of the previous century did. She was a fair, barefoot girl in a long,

The Black Hostelry was built into the south nave aisle of the ruined medieval hospital.

white gown who occasionally joined them during late night fire-drills, standing alone in the Norman doorway by the first floor fire exit. Could this angelic apparition be the infamous daughter of 17th century headmaster, William Pamply? If so, she was certainly no angel. The 'loose-living' Mistress Pamply shared the male boarders' accommodation, long before girls were admitted to study, and conducted 'a dauncinge school' after hours. Her father was dismissed in 1609 for besmirching the establishment's reputation and it barely survived the scandal.

Elizabeth's Deanery ghosts were much more unpleasant. As her mother was an invalid and her father often away on business, she was obliged to walk alone to Evensong in the cathedral. The Deanery's front exit led to Oyster Lane beside the Dean's Meadow, overhung with wind-torn, whispering trees. The back exit led through a claustrophobic yard to the unlit Firmary Lane, ruined, roofless nave of the monastery hospital, which had developed into a cul-de-sac. Clergy homes were built into both sides of its former arched aisles. On the left was the haunted Black Hostelry where visiting Benedictine monks once lodged, and on the right, the haunted Walsingham House, '. . . and either ghost might issue out; not to mention our own ghost who had probably walked out of the house behind me and at any moment might lay his hand on my shoulder as we went along.'

According to Elizabeth, The Black Hostelry contained 'something rather nasty'. She knew of a guest who had rushed outside in terror. Walsingham House - now used as the Kings' School's Choir House - had been Alan of Walsingham's 14th century pad 'The Painted Chamber'. Before Elizabeth's time, an internal upstairs wall had been knocked down to reveal a man's skeleton. The bones were buried and the building exorcised, but she seldom walked down the lane 'without horrible thoughts of what it must feel like to be walled up'. The clergy family who lived there in Elizabeth's time, were 'weighed down with a sense of misery in a certain part of the house'. More than a century later, a house mistress who occupied the top floor with her family, discovered that her baby and toddler both cried hysterically in one bedroom but slept peacefully through the night in another.

Sir Walter Scott's famous poem, Marmian, relates the tale of nun, Constance de Beverley of Whitby Abbey, who was walled up as punishment for

Powcher's Hall (on the left) home of Canon Ratcliff between 1947 and 1958.

Firmary Lane entrance to The Choir House, alias Walsingham House, alias The Painted Chamber. The cat is real.

Powcher's Hall, now a clergy home, is built into the north nave aisle of the ruined medieval hospital.

breaking her vows with a bold but fickle knight. Perhaps something similar occurred at Ely. Walsingham offered the use of his house to the female relatives of sick or senile monks, while they visited their loved ones in the adjacent hospital. Picture the scene: a hot-blooded young monk on route to his bimonthly bloodletting session in nearby Powcher's Hall, catches a glimpse of a visitor's slim ankle, and follows her to The Painted Chamber, where they are later discovered *in flagrante delicto*. Was he walled-up at the scene of passion as an example to others?

If only fate had let him glimpse that tempting ankle after his bloodletting session, there might have been a different ending to the tale. Bloodletting was a monastic solution to the problem of celibacy. A lower blood level was believed to subdue sensual desire. Documentary evidence suggests that as much as three pints of blood were taken by leeches at each session, enough for a monk to lose consciousness. At Soutra, one of Britain's most important medieval hospitals near Edinburgh, blood dumps found preserved in clay seem to confirm the practice.

Elizabeth's keen nose for ghosts failed to sniff out the grinning monk who peeps from a small back window of Powcher's Hall, location of the bloodletting sessions, and the following few days of rest and recuperation. Monks relished this brief respite from the grinding monastic routine, enjoying nights of uninterrupted sleep, a brief glimpse of the outside world and a chance to taste better food. The infirmary menu for August 1388 included beef, mutton, pork, veal, pullets, capons, fish, eggs, milk, cream, mustard, cheese and spices. No wonder he grins.

Eleven year old Margaret E. moved to Powcher's Hall in 1947 when her mother became housekeeper to bachelor Canon Ratcliff, Professor of Divinity at Ely. Not long after their arrival, she was sitting in a window seat on the second floor with her new friend Rani, the Siamese cat, when they heard footsteps coming up the stairs. Both turned towards the sound, but as nobody appeared or answered Margaret's call, she went downstairs to investigate. Her mother was baking in the kitchen and the Professor was out. One day as Mrs E. was hanging out washing in the garden, the grinning monk appeared at a small window beside the back door. Assuming that her employer had a visitor, she rushed inside and put on the kettle. Clerical gentlemen often called unexpectedly and she always made tea. When she appeared in the study with a loaded tray set for two, the Canon was alone but not surprised. He heard things too.

All three of them would stop to listen as light footsteps paced along the upstairs corridor towards the first floor drawing room, whose windows overlooked the garden. All three heard the drawing room door open and shut. Once a monk dressed in white appeared in Margaret's bedroom and spoke to her in a strange language. She described him to the professor who recognised the dress of a certain order not usually seen at Ely - but it was a long time ago and she has forgotten the order's name. When the professor was away, Margaret's grandmother came to stay. A commotion on the top floor during the night sent the three females diving beneath their bedclothes. 'Take what you want and go!' shouted Grandma. In the morning they went upstairs together, expecting a mess - but everything looked the same.

In 1958 Canon Ratcliff left Ely to become Regius Professor of Divinity at Cambridge. Mrs E. and Margaret went with him, though both were reluctant to leave the familiar ghosts of Powcher's Hall.

5 More Monks, a Serving Wench and some Spooky Footprints

Eighty years after the Goudge family left Ely, Elizabeth's attic bedroom had become part of a second floor flat, used by incoming clergy families while they awaited permanent accommodation. During the summer of 1990 it was occupied by the recently appointed cathedral precentor, the Rev Stephen Shipley, his wife Rosie and their young children. On the night Mrs Shipley experienced the wandering monk, she had decided to sleep alone in a little room at the end of the first floor corridor. She was not feeling well, and her previous night's rest had been disturbed by her young son, who was sharing his parents' bedroom. Her following night's rest would be disturbed by something worse.

Rosie Shipley wrote of her experience in *Ely Cathedral News*, April 1992: 'It was during the second or third night on my own that I was suddenly awoken by the sound of approaching footsteps . . . suddenly I was gripped with fear and, I'm ashamed to say, I burrowed under the bedclothes.' She lay frozen, heart pounding, unable to call out. Eventually the sensation subsided. She put on the light and read for a while to calm herself, then went back to sleep. Some time later, it happened again. 'I was awoken by the distinct sound of footsteps . . . I could hear the vibration of items on the piano with each step. . . again I was seized with terror, again I dived under the bedclothes and again I experienced those nightmarish sensations.'

She wanted to run upstairs to her husband but the corridor was too dark. So she put on the light and read some more - and so the night passed, but the experience was still vivid the following day. 'Imagine, then, the impact that a passage in Elizabeth Goudge's autobiography had on me when I happened to come across it less than a week later . . . While the external details were different - I had only heard footsteps while she saw a figure - I felt that Elizabeth Goudge could not have described my own experience better.' The Shipleys moved as soon as possible.

A few years earlier, a newly appointed King's School teacher spent a month in the same flat. Coming downstairs on the first morning, he passed a pretty serving wench in a dark dress, white apron and cap, carrying a jug of steaming water along the landing, but as he turned for another look, she disappeared through the end wall. No one took much notice of his tale. Such happenings are ten a penny at the College. Perhaps it was this same maidservant who came up the park on the Tuesday morning following the death of Princess Diana in 1996. A local business man remembers passing an attractive young woman in a long dark skirt and sparkling white blouse, on his way to the photocopy shop on Broad Street. He is sure of the date, as he was going to pick up a notice announcing that his shops would be closed on the day of the funeral. When he looked round, she was gone. The path leads to the Porta, but bears right just before the archway, passing the Oyster Lane entrance to The Deanery, on its way towards town.

One night in 1944, during the Second World War, young Les Oakey and his pal took this same short cut to town, but soon they wished they had not. There were no lights because of the blackout, but opposite Oyster Lane they could just make out the shape of a little Jewish evacuee boy called Schwartz, cowering beside the cloister wall. He grabbed hold of Les and pointed towards an open space at the top of Firmary Lane, former site of the medieval Chapter House where monastery business was conducted. A narrow passageway, called the Slype, connected this medieval office building with the south transept - and was one of very few places where monks could meet and exchange opinions. Apparently they still do. All three boys saw two monks, arguing and gesticulating, and all three took to their heels, through the Porta to the Jews' Free School in The Gallery. (The school had been evacuated from London for the duration of war, and was located in Old Hereward Hall opposite the Porta.)

Forty years later, school teacher, Tony Ransome, took the short cut one evening at about 6 pm. As he reached the open space, a robed figure emerged from a small

The arched gateway used by Richard's monks, is much frequented by local people.

doorway in the south transept and crossed the path in front of him. 'Good evening' said Tony politely, but the figure ignored him and disappeared through another doorway on the far side of Firmary Lane. In December 2000, a BBC security officer called Danny was guarding television equipment outside the south transept on the night before the cathedral's Millennium concert, and watched a similar figure take the same journey between the same two bricked-up doorways.

The college path winds between the monks' graveyard (sensibly located beside their hospital) and the garden wall of Powcher's Hall (where the grinning monk peers from his window), and curves around the Lady Chapel towards the North Range buildings that form the college boundary. At the far corner, a smaller path turns right to the Almonry Gate and emerges on the High Street, not far from Johnsons the Cleaners, a shop now occupying the site of the Porta Monachorum or Monks' Gate. Perhaps the bashful brother who lurks around the back has a dirty habit - or a raging thirst. 'Naughty monks' would slip through the gate at dusk, and cross the Market Square to sample strong ale at the White Hart. Monastic ale 'was so weak that the pigs would not drink of it'. The monks were not keen on it either.

The College path turns left by the Lady Chapel - the very spot where Richard Whitehand's two monks turned right - and leads through the arch by the public toilets towards the Sacrist's Gate. Perhaps it was one of these cowled brothers who left two deep footprints in the freshly fallen snow of the Sacrist's yard during the cold winter of 1991. The Sacrist's Gate and adjacent building - now occupied by Octagon Studio dance school - were then in use as Ely Museum. Attendant, Liz

Two footprints were discovered in the snow behind the high wall on the left of the Sacrist's Gate.

```
|_____|_____|_____|
     |         |         |
     |         |  WALL   |
     |_____|_____|_____
          |         |         |
          |         |         |
```

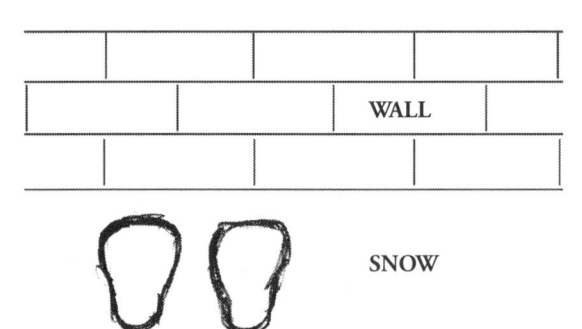

  ◯ ◯
        SNOW

'The footprints looked like the soles of old fashioned sandals - wider at the toe and narrower at the heel, but without shape, and about size six,' said Liz Nardone.

Nardone, unlocked the back door for a quick smoke soon after arriving at 9 am and discovered the roughly oval shaped prints facing the wall on the left of the doorway, where perhaps an earlier entrance had opened into the yard. 'I looked up to see if anything was dripping that might have cause the marks, but there wasn't', said Liz. 'Then I tiptoed around the yard to see if any footprints led in from the back gate, but it was locked and the snow was smooth.'

The prints - sketched on a scrap of paper by Liz before they melted - resembled a 16th century leather sole that was excavated from the river during the Broad Street archaeological dig ten years later, and shown on Channel Four's Time Team programme. Liz took her camera to work for the rest of the winter but there was no more snow and no sign of the mysterious bare toed visitor.

Perhaps he got cold feet and moved next door to popular clothes shop, Jumpers, located in the Goldsmith's Tower, where

High Street shop, Jumpers, was a monastic workshop or store - possibly a wine store. The Bishops had their own vineyards and produced wine in times when the climate was warmer, though the best monastery wine was imported.

brightly striped woollies fling themselves off shelves during the night. Former manager, Kate Marshall, was aware of a presence almost as soon as the shop opened in 1989. She would arrive each morning to find piles of knitwear swept onto the floor. It happened in daytime too, in front of staff and customers. Kate saw the probable culprit in two different places, though she never saw him move between them. Sometimes he stood at the back by the changing rooms, in what used to be a yard. At other times, he stood near the shop doorway, beside the counter. The short, skinny monk kept his face hidden inside his hood, but Kate felt he was young and sad. Was he mourning the loss of his close-knit community?

Steeple Gate, near the end of the college path, connects the High Street with St Cross Green, a popular grassy picnic spot that evolved from one of the parish graveyards. In medieval times, when the ground was full up, old bones would be taken out and stacked in a bone-house which stood on the site of the present Steeple Gate trinket shop and tearoom. By the 19th century this practice had died out, so skulls and blackened bones were left to moulder on the surface until a new cemetery opened on the edge of the city in 1855. An earlier entrance gate was used by medieval pilgrims, drawn irresistibly towards the abbey shrines. The present Tudor gateway is used by modern tourists, drawn irresistibly towards the cheerful sound of clattering cups and saucers from the first floor tearoom - and puzzled by the sound of smashing cups and saucers, hurled into the sink by the resident poltergeist in the second floor kitchen.

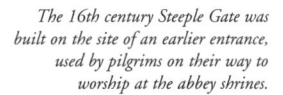

The 16th century Steeple Gate was built on the site of an earlier entrance, used by pilgrims on their way to worship at the abbey shrines.

6 The Commuting Ghosts of Silver Street Cottages

Three timber-framed terraced cottages near The Fountain public house in Silver Street were originally the family wing, central hall and servant wing of a late medieval hall house that was partitioned in the 19th century. This important site, right opposite the main monastery gateway, the Porta, suggests it was the home of a local bigwig, perhaps a prosperous merchant or cathedral high official. The buxom matron who sits in the upper room of the first cottage, holding glittering jewels towards the light of the window in heavily ringed fingers may have been his wife.

Silver Street Cottages were originally a single late medieval hall house.

The upper room was a private solar where ladies of the house could retire to gossip and sew, and would have occupied the entire first floor of the family wing. Exquisite 15th century paintings survive along the original fireplace wall, which is now part of a corridor connecting the present tenant's bedroom and bathroom. On the vermilion tinted wall opposite the bathroom door, a painted white dove outlined in black is amazingly well preserved inside a small alcove, with motto *"Deale Justlye"*, inscribed above. On either side of the alcove are much fainter paintings of a white peacock with the motto *'Be not Proud"* and a heron with the motto *'Bear no Malice'*. Both paintings are surrounded by swirling foliage and bordered by the remains of an inscription reading *'Be sober at . . .'*

These rare domestic wall paintings would have been executed by one of many itinerant artists who had discovered a gap in the medieval market, and travelled round the countryside decorating rich men's homes. Their designs were copied from embroidered tapestries, accessible only to the very rich indeed, that hung on the walls of palaces, great houses and ecclesiastical buildings. Wallpaper was invented later, and slapped layer upon layer, over the 'old-fashioned' paintings, unintentionally preserving them. In 1987 an architect working for Cambridge Cottage Improvement Society peeled off more than forty layers and revealed the hidden splendour.

No paintings survive on the other three walls of the solar, now part of a bedroom where the ghost and her jewellery were spotted by an Australian friend of the restored cottage's first tenant. The startled guest shot up in bed to inspect the midnight caller, while her husband snored on peacefully beside her. The present tenant has seen nothing, but her son's cat, Tuesday, did when it came to stay for the 2000 AD Millennium weekend. She tells the tale: 'It was after midnight when I returned from the bathroom and Tuesday was standing quite still on the end of my antique sleigh bed, with her front paws on the foot board, staring into the corner where the ghost is supposed to sit. Every bit of fur stood on end, even the little white bit under her chin. After about five minutes she shook herself and jumped down. Then I got into bed and went to sleep. Tuesday had stayed in the house before and since but that was the only time it happened.'

Vine Cottage, next door, is named after wall paintings that are even earlier than those of the aptly named Dove Cottage. A naturalistic grapevine design covers the plaster work between the timber studs of one of the sitting room's walls, and would have served as an imitation tapestry backdrop for the raised dining platform of the open hall. The original tenant and his family would have dined at a long trestle table, in front of the decoration and beneath the canopy whose joist holes are still visible. The dining area faced a doorway that led to the servants' wing, but now contains a tall corner cupboard. Sometimes, an affluent looking, jovial gentleman in black knee length breeches and black stockings appears through the cupboard and joins the early 21st century occupant of Vine Cottage on her chintzy chesterfield.

As Chris Wall watches television from one end of the chesterfield, her uninvited guest sits down at the other. He crosses his legs, taps his foot nervously and fiddles with

The vine-scroll ornamentation in Vine Cottage is very early domestic wall painting. The mortise at the top of the third timber stud from the left suggests that a canopy once projected into the room, above the painting, long before a second floor was added.

a chain that hangs round his neck with a small metal cup on the end - an indication that he might be a wine merchant, and the husband of next door's matron. The agitated apparition seems to be watching the cupboard, as though he expects someone else to appear. Although they often share the chesterfield, she always feels apprehensive when he appears, though he is not threatening and only stays for a couple of minutes.

When Chris came to Ely as a carer for the Social Services, she lived briefly in Dove Cottage before moving next door, but never saw the merchant's wife - though she used to lie awake in the solar bedroom, listening to the rustle of silken skirts along the corridor. She is more familiar with the phantom family who flit back and forth through the blocked-up doorways of all three cottages as though it were still a single home - but imagines they belong to a later century. Whenever she pops next door to drink tea with her un-psychic neighbour, the phantom father follows through the wall and waits below the fragment of painted frieze that survives above the living room fireplace (formerly the hall house parlour). Chris calls him Adrian, not a name that would necessarily spring to mind for a 16th century ghost, but one chosen at random by the tenant of the third cottage, Number 11. (The servants' wing has no wall painting and therefore no name.)

Jo Odell-Rourke moved into Number 11 with her husband Rocky, in April 1993 when he became head chef of the King's School, who lease the cottage. The neighbours met when they arrived home at the same time one day, and simultaneously inserted keys into their locks. Jo opened the conversation. with an enquiry about the crash she heard behind her 16th century fireplace that backs onto Chris's fireplace, earlier that morning. Chris replied that it was only her ghost knocking things over. Jo exclaimed 'Oh, you've got them too!' and invited her round for tea to compare notes. She had already experienced 'the phantom of the fireplace' while phoning her mother, soon after she moved in. 'A hanging basket of potpourri that I'd hung from a beam over the fireplace started swinging - faster and faster - until it flicked right off its hook and smashed to the floor, spilling potpourri all over the hearth. I told Mum and she said it must be a plane going over.'

Their descriptions of Adrian matched. He was thirtyish, blonde, about five foot nine and usually wore a white shirt with military trousers. Jo saw him hurrying across the dining room towards the side window as she sat on the settee feeding her first baby on a warm summer evening. She mistook him for her husband who was about the same height and colouring and usually wore a white chef's jacket, but as she turned to speak, he walked through the side window (which used to be a door) into the garden. Babies' eyes generally only focus if they are looking at something in particular, so Jo is pretty certain that the baby saw him too. Soon there was a second baby and the first one had learned to talk. Whenever the door squeaked, he would look up and say 'Daddy coming', but it was often only Adrian on his way to the garden or through the party-wall to Vine Cottage.

When Chris sees Adrian in the garden, he seems hazy and dresses like a Cromwellian soldier, though the tied-back, shoulder-length hairstyle seems wrong. Indoors he looks more solid. Upstairs she sees him leaning against a chest of drawers, dressed casually in a white shirt with floppy sleeves, leather jerkin, sacking pants and bare feet, as she lies in bed beneath the cottage's magnificent crown-post roof. The great rough timber beams were thickly encrusted with soot when they were exposed by 20th century builders, who removed the second floor to open up the first floor bedroom - and complained that their tools moved about during tea breaks. The soot shows that a central hearth heated the main hall, long before the two upper rooms were added - and perhaps explains the faint smell of wood smoke that lingers.

'Sometimes when I'm too tired to read', says Chris, ' I get into bed and stretch out, yawn like crazy, and turn out the light. Then, just as I'm getting settled, the pressure of the bed changes. I always lie in the centre but it's a big bed and there's room on either side. I curl up on my left side with left leg curled up, right leg straight on left side, and just prior to dropping off, the bed sinks slightly as if someone is sitting on the bed, then lying full length next to me, and settling into position, rather like my ex-husband only lighter, but it's not sexual. There's just a comforting feeling of "thank goodness I can lie down". I don't feel like moving so I say "goodnight" and there's a sigh.'

Adrian's wife stays downstairs with the three children. She is about five foot two with long, dark hair. The older boy is about ten, slender like his parents with a funny pudding basin haircut, sackcloth shirt and muddy trousers. Chris see him in the garden with a girl of about four, who has a reddish tint to her hair. She wears a long sleeved smock, wipes her hands down it and always looks dirty. They are both barefoot. 'I've seen her pick my things up and throw them around. Once she threw a plant pot containing my money tree, that stood on the corner of the window ledge. It landed by the coffee table in six pieces, but the plant wasn't damaged. I asked why she did that but she never looks at me. I think she's jealous of her baby brother. I haven't seen him but heard him crying one Sunday evening in my bathroom that juts out into Number 11.'

Jo heard the baby too. She thought it was her own baby, and rushed upstairs, only to discover him fast asleep. There was a strange baby in an old fashioned cot, crying and bouncing up and down in an all-in-one suit. 'He looked at me tearfully then faded.' When Jo's younger boy was four he used to say he was going upstairs to play with the boys. 'Once I found him lying on his back on the landing with his feet against the wall, giggling and talking to someone who he said was his friend. After we moved he used to say "I wonder how the boys are?"'

The Odell-Rourkes moved in 1998 when Rocky was promoted, and the King's School turned Number 11 into a sanatorium. But two years before they left, Anglia Television came to film a programme about the haunted cottages. 'The ghosts were upset,' says Jo. 'They thought they were being mocked because the cameraman - tall, blonde and dressed as Adrian in a white frilly shirt and knee breeches - appeared to walk through the wall. They used lots of dry ice and I must admit it looked very good on camera but Adrian didn't appreciate it.'

Number 11's squeaky door.

7 The Cromwells, a Fenland Legend and some Galloping Hooves

At the beginning of the 13th century Alan of Walsingham supervised the construction of a stone bridge and causeway across the marshes that separated Ely from its neighbouring island of Stuntney, so that produce from the monastery's outlying farms could be brought to the isle by land. Now the busy A142 leaves Ely along this causeway, climbing Stuntney Hill towards Newmarket and bisecting monastic land that was farmed after the Reformation by the Steward family. Horses trotting up the hill shy and side-step at the spot where the new road crosses an older one that led between the Steward home, Stuntney Old Hall, on the left of the hill, and Stuntney village on the right. Motorists swerve and sound their horns at a whispy young woman who strides across the road, swishing her long skirts and swinging her basket, without looking left or right. Tradition says she is Kathryn, second wife of William Steward, mother of Thomas and Elizabeth, and maternal grandmother of Oliver Cromwell.

Stuntney Old Hall, which has since fallen down, was drawn by Henry Baines about 1860.

The window of the haunted bedroom with the Tithe Office doorway below at Oliver Cromwell's house.

The lintel post and frame of the blocked up doorway in the haunted bedroom

The Reformation was a godsend for opportunists like the Stewards. Elizabeth and Thomas's great-uncle Robert, who was Ely's last Catholic Prior, switched religions and became its first Protestant Dean. Their grandfather and father took-over profitable monastic land which was later inherited by Thomas, who died childless in 1636, leaving most of his estate and the position 'Farmer of the Tithes' to his only nephew, Oliver. Elizabeth had married Robert Cromwell of Hinchingbrook House, Huntingdon, producing the single surviving son in 1599, as well as seven daughters.

The upwardly mobile Cromwell's new estate included a 'fine parsonage house' next to St Mary's Church in the centre of Ely, and he moved in at once with his wife, mother, two unmarried sisters, four sons and two daughters. His new position allowed him to collect tithes (or taxes), from which he was obliged to pay a fixed amount to the Dean and Chapter, but anything left over was his to keep. This income helped him to become MP for Cambridge and eventually, Lord Protector of England. Two more daughters were born in the house, increasing the number of Cromwell women living there to eight, but it must be one of the older generation of females who patrols the corridors with a bunch of keys at her waist. The brooding male presence is surely Oliver himself.

The last cleric to occupy the 13th century parsonage was Canon Neil Munt, vicar of Ely between 1974 and 1986. In April 1979, he and his wife Joan, invited a couple of friends to stay the weekend and put them in the 17th century west wing bedroom, directly above Cromwell's former tithe office that overlooked the courtyard. Marion woke in the night when Brian got up to visit the en suite bathroom, and remained awake after he had returned and gone back to sleep. Without knowing how it happened, she found herself standing in a corner of the room. There was a doorway in front of her that should have been on the right. Her bare feet touched rough wooden floorboards, though she knew the room was carpeted. A man's strong grip held her upper arms. Her hands pushed against his chest, feeling the rough leather of his jerkin, though she could not see his face. She felt a deep bond between them, sensing his physical power and determined personality, and knew he had made a decision that would change the course of both their lives - but was it her present life or that of a person in another time? She was not afraid of him but for him and for the changes his decision would bring. 'In my mind, but not, I think, spoken aloud was the phrase "Tis not my way" said again and again. Yet I accepted that the decision had been made. His grip on my arms was tight but I had no thought that he intended to hurt me. It was expression of his determination to pursue his course of action.'

Marion wanted to wake her husband but could not. She was part of two separate existences but could reach neither. Suddenly she was free. The door faded. She returned to bed, cold and tired, and slept until morning. Her arms ached when she woke and there were red finger marks around both, stronger on the left. She showed Brian but didn't say anything as she needed to think. Later, when she told him, he went upstairs to examine the room and noticed the old lintel post and frame where the original doorway had been plastered over. The existing 18th century doorway and gallery corridor that led from it, were built onto a 17th century two-storey extension that had been added to the rear of 14th and 15th century areas of the house. Over lunch Brian told the Munts, their daughter Alison and her friend, about Marion's experience and they all examined the fading marks. Alison knew the room was haunted as she often heard footsteps in the corridor and a door opening and shutting. Alison and Marion both discovered that several years previously on separate occasions, they had each seen a woman in a long, dark dress going up the stairs but neither had liked to mention it.

Kate Marshall and her sister Angela saw the woman too, when they stayed at the vicarage with Rev. Jack Bagley (vicar of Ely from 1963 to 1974) and Mrs Bagley, who were friends of their parents. 'My sister and I stayed with the Bagleys for a few days during the summer holidays. We were giggling and chatting in the night and had we been at home father would have shouted at us, but we fell silent when a lady wearing a long blue dress with keys at the waist came into the room. She had dark hair, no hat, and just looked at us, turned and went out.' Kate saw her again a few years later while staying at the vicarage to look after the Bagley's grandson whose parents were in Hong Kong. The Bagleys had seen her too. Kate says 'I can't make up my mind whether it is us drifting into their time or them drifting into ours, but it does happen.'

Three days after Marian's traumatic experience, she sat down to type an account of the event, but had forgotten her captor's name and the nature of his decision - though both had been clear to her at the time. Who was he? Why was he agitated? What was the decision he had made? If her nocturnal visitor had been Cromwell, the decision that caused him such unease may have been whether to sign the 1649 death warrant of King

Charles Ist. His signature on the document was only one of 57, yet perhaps the most significant. The Fenland legend of *The Grey Goose Feather* tells of the king's escape from Oxford in April 1646, his flight into East Anglia dressed as a clergyman - and of Cromwell's indecision.

The legend combines myth with fact. King Charles did flee from Oxford to Norfolk and may have stayed overnight at the White Swan in Downham Market disguised as a clergyman - but according to eye witness, Dr Michael Hudson, the royal chaplain who accompanied the king, they stayed a few miles down the road at Snore (Snowre) Hall, Fordham, with the Catholic Skipwith family, who were strong royalists. The Hall was built on a slight hill surrounded by ploughed land, leading to its curious name, which comes from the Saxon 'snare' meaning the distance between two furrows of ploughed land. It was unusual to be able to plough so near the sea in Norfolk.

According to the *Sunday Telegraph*, Snore Hall is haunted. In October, 1996, the newspaper reported 'Heritage Minister, Iain Sproat, is wearing a worried look. The reason: he has discovered that his country home is overrun with ghosts.' Apparently Mr Sproat, ex-member of Parliament for Harwich and owner of the hall between 1987 and 2003, was sitting alone, reading, in his 15th century pile when a shadowy figure entered the room and hovered by his chair. Local yokels know this figure as 'The Dark Shadow', a catholic priest who runs from the building on moonlit nights, specially chosen by bounty hunters so they could see their victims.

Snore (Snowre) Hall is the oldest, domestic brick building in Norfolk. The 'w' was added later when 'snore' became considered a coarse word, but then dropped again for authenticity in the 20th century. Snore village was mentioned in the Domesday Book but has since disappeared.

In the uncertain times of the 16th and 17th centuries when the national religion changed according to the whim of whoever occupied the throne, a succession of priests visited the Skipwiths who continued to follow 'the old faith' in spite of adversity. The priest in residence performed mass and baptisms in a secret chapel, hidden in the roof space, which contained a thirty foot bolt hole to the ground floor. (Presumably an escaping priest would be obliged to shin down a rope.) Catholics travelled long distances to worship at this remote place and brought their children to learn the scriptures and be baptised. A family retainer who put the children to bed is rumoured to perform the same service for present day young guests, who have been known to ask their mothers: 'Do I know that old lady who tucked me in?'

Secret passageways and hidey-holes were built into the Hall walls by England's greatest creator of priest-holes, Nicholas Owen, a Jesuit who was a mason and carpenter by trade. During the day he would perform general building work to fool the servants. At night he dug holes, chipped through stonework and sawed wooden panels to create secret rooms that were known only to himself and the Skipwiths. It must have been difficult work, especially as Owen was a dwarf. His stomach was held together by a metal plate because of a hernia, and he walked with a limp. The failure of the Gunpowder Plot in 1605 focused attention on Catholics, and he was captured and tortured to death in the Tower of London without revealing any of his secrets.

Owen had been dead for more than forty years when King Charles and Dr Hudson pounded up Snore Hall's driveway on their fast, thoroughbred horses - and they had been dead for more than three hundred and fifty, when Mr Sproat heard

Ghostly hooves pounded up the driveway of Snore Hall, but nothing was there.

hooves galloping along the same driveway, but nothing was there. The Hall lies isolated, though right beside the main road between Ely and the once prosperous seaport of King's Lynn. If the doomed king intended to flee abroad, he changed his mind after holding his last Council of War in the King's Chamber on 30th April, 1646, and decided to join his men at Huntingdon. His last hope was the Scottish Army at Newark, but he needed a local guide to lead him across the Fens.

The legend says that he chose Mucky Porter, a disreputable rogue from Southery. When the royal chaplain voiced his distrust, the shifty fellow pulled a grey goose feather from his pocket, snapped it in two and gave half to the king. 'I am a Fenlander,' he said, pocketing the other half, 'and now must help His Majesty.' All members of the Fenland brotherhood carried the feathers, which had only to be shown to brothers in times of need to guarantee help. Mucky took his fine gentlemen to Southery and swapped their fine horses for two old nags and their satin clothes for sackcloth. Then he led them across remote fens to Huntingdon and the royalist forces.

But the king was obliged to surrender at Newark. He stood trial, was found guilty and sentenced to death. On the night before the execution, Dr Hudson took the grey goose feather to Cromwell and said 'His Majesty does not ask for pardon, but only that he is afforded that due to one who holds this token.' Cromwell sat up all night staring at the feather, and perhaps muttering 'Tis not my way' - for he was a Fenlander too, and knew the tradition. But the next morning the king lost his head and Cromwell lost his Fen soldiers, who threw down their feathers in disgust and went home.

When Mucky Porter was a very old man, some gentlemen came looking for him in Southery. 'Are you Mr Mucky Porter?' they enquired. 'It depends who's asking,' said Mucky. 'I'm asking', replied the most flamboyant. 'Mr Porter helped my father escape from Cromwell's men and I have come to reward him with land.' So Mucky went to the stable and fetched his posh horse - a descendent of the two he obtained earlier - and rode with the royal party to Methwold Fen, where the Crown owned a great deal of boggy land that had recently been transformed by drainage into rich, black, peaty soil. 'Here we are,' said the king. 'How much would you like?'

'Well' said Mucky, 'I'll have from that barn over there, to that ditch right over there, to that tree in the distance. How much do you think I've got?'

'Mr. Porter', said King Charles II, 'I think you have several acres'. And ever since then, the land has been called the Methwold Severals and has always been farmed by a Porter.

8 Ely Tourist Information Centre, Soldiers, an Actress and more Galloping Hooves

'Cromwell's ghost untied my shoes!' exclaimed the front page headline of the *Ely Standard* on 3rd December 1998. The shoes in question belonged to Chris Jones, who works as a guide for East Cambs District Council. He was sitting at a desk in his office at the back of Oliver Cromwell's House, ten years after it opened as Ely Tourist Information Centre.

A strong breeze playing around his trouser legs made him glance down. His left shoelace was undone so he bent down and tied it. A few minutes later the breeze returned. The right shoelace was undone. He bent down and tied it. The breeze blew again. His left shoe lace was undone again. Later Chris told an *Ely Standard* reporter: 'I did not believe in ghosts. I am level headed but this was really strange. After it happened a third time I left the room and one of the staff thought I looked pale. I can't explain why it happened because there is no practical reason. The laces were tied properly. It is hard to describe the draught. It was like something gently brushing my leg. Nothing like this has ever happened to me before.'

Chris's room is in the original 13th century part of the house and always feels cold. It probably served as a larder for the adjacent kitchen, one of eight rooms furnished in Cromwellian style and open to the public. Here, visitors can view the 15th century fireplace where Mrs Cromwell cooked over an open fire. Models of the foodstuffs she might have used are displayed on the sturdy oak table, whiteish-purple carrots, cheese similar to Stilton, dried fruit, nuts, and bags of vegetables that were suspended and boiled alongside the meat. Herbs hang from the rafters, and were used in medicines, as well as for cooking.

A lucky visitor might even catch a glimpse of the good woman herself - as Liz Jordan did one morning when she worked in the house in 2002. Liz came in through the yard and along the back corridor. 'As I opened the kitchen door, I saw the bottom half of a person in a long, blue skirt disappearing into a mist by the wall near the fireplace. I shrugged it off as my imagination but then went on a ghost walk around Ely on the following Friday night. When we reached Oliver Cromwell's House, the guide mentioned

Mrs Cromwell's kitchen is in the oldest part of Oliver Cromwell's House (on the left of the photograph) and overlooks St Mary's Churchyard. The gravestones have been moved into neat rows around the church.

a blue lady. *I did not know about her* - but at that point, realised I'd seen her.'

Liz had already experienced another phenomenon in the house, while working there four years earlier. She arrived early and was at her desk in the upstairs office when she heard heavy footsteps crossing the landing. She assumed they belonged to her supervisor, Jason, who wore big boots - until he arrived twenty minutes later, taking his coat off as he entered. At the end of the corridor lies the haunted bedroom. Its eerie atmosphere has abated since Marion and Brian slept there - a waxwork Oliver lies dying in a reproduction 17th century bed and an electric spectre lurks behind a curtain - though according to the *Ely Standard* ' . . . earlier this year, a workman repairing pipes bolted from the room and refused to return after witnessing ghostly goings-on'.

Within days of the shoelace skirmish another member of staff spotted a grey figure in the haunted bedroom as he checked the building before locking up. He called out that the house was closing, and then went downstairs. The girl on the desk told him all the visitors had gone so they returned upstairs together. The figure was gone too.

At the beginning of the Civil War, Cromwell picked out 'honest sober Christians' for Parliament's New Model Army, from among local men gathered on St Mary's Green in front of his house. The soldiers were self-reliant, tough and stoical, all qualities nurtured by the region's isolation from the rest of the country - a quirk of geography that also preserved the purity of their British stock. The short, dark, sturdy Fenmen had spherical skulls which, emphasised by their cropped haircuts, led to the nickname 'Roundheads.' Cromwell said he preferred 'a plain russet-coated captain, that knows what he fights for, and loves what he knows, than what you call a gentleman and nothing else.' His troops were 'well equipped, well horsed and well paid'. They were well trained too. Cromwell drilled them in state-of-the-art battlefield tactics on nearby Palace Green, a triangular stretch of grass situated between the Cathedral, the Bishop's Palace and The Chantry.

The 18th century Chantry house replaced an earlier Chantry Chapel, where four chaplains lived and prayed daily for the soul of Bishop Northwold, for which they received twenty marks a year.

The present Chantry - an elegant 18th century house - replaced the medieval Chantry Chapel, founded in 1250 by Bishop Northwold. During the 1970s, Bunty Jones used to baby-sit for Mr and Mrs T. Bristol who still live there, though their children have grown up and gone. One evening, as she watched television around midnight and waited for the Bristols to return, the room turned icy cold and she was unable to rise from her chair. Rough, swearing, male voices shouted from the next room. Heavy boots marched about. Doors banged. After about fifteen minutes the noise faded and the room became warmer. Bunty was able to move again and raced upstairs to the children but they were fast asleep. As soon as the Bristols returned, she left and never went back. Later, she related her experiences to Mrs Bristol, who was not surprised. Her husband heard voices too. The lady who inhabited the house before them, said the voices belonged to Cromwell's soldiers. The Chapel became a dwelling after the Reformation. She claimed that at the beginning of the Civil War it was raided by Roundheads, who were mopping up pockets of local royalist resistance and seizing weapons and money for the army.

King Charles II is believed to have stayed with Bishop Gunning at his palace, opposite The Chantry, when the monarchy was restored soon after Cromwell's death. In those days, the powerful Bishops of Ely occupied responsible positions of state. Bishop Gunning was a political adviser to the new king, but in his spare time enjoyed gardening. He planted a plane tree that would take 350 years to become the largest and

The biggest plane tree in England is overlooked by the Bishop's Palace, in its turn overlooked by Ely Cathedral.

oldest in England. Perhaps master and servant strolled beside the tender sapling to discuss state business in privacy. But why was the king in Ely?

Jean Eames, great-granddaughter of George Peck, who founded Peck's the Ironmongers in the late 19th century, thinks she knows the answer. A story passed down through her family relates that - true to his nickname - the 'Merrie Monarch' was attending the races at nearby Newmarket, and drove over to Ely with his current mistress, Nell Gwynne, to inspect a young race horse, recently born on the Bishop's New Barns estate. It was King James I who began the royal tradition of racing at Newmarket in the early 1600s, but it was his grandson Charles who made the town famous, riding his own horses there in 1671, under his other nickname 'Old Rowley'.

If King Charles stayed at the Bishop's Palace, 'pretty, witty Nell' certainly did not. Jean's story suggests that she lodged rather less grandly at a private house in the High Street, whose ground floor was converted to become Pizza Express at the beginning of the 21st century. At the end of the 19th century, the Peck family took-over the three storey building from Wilton's Boot and Shoe shop, and received an unexpected bonus. Miss Gwynne's ghost reclined in the first floor window-seat, gazing down the High Street in the direction of Palace Green. But when the elegant, two-storey, mullioned, bay window was replaced in the 1920s with 'something a bit more modern', it was final curtains for the spirited scrubber, orange-seller, actress, king's mistress and probably England's top commuting ghost. Nell has been spotted in Edinburgh, London, Newmarket, Northampton, St Albans, Windsor, York . . . . .

Nell Gwynne was reputed to recline in the elegant, bay window of a shop in Ely High Street, drawn by Henry Baines about 1860.

Developers of Pizza Express replaced the 'modern' early 20th century window with a 21st century interpretation of the original.

Owning racehorses was a rich man's hobby. The Bishops of Ely were certainly rich, but whether King Charles ever visited their New Barns estate is unknown. King George IV did as Prince Regent, but that was a hundred years later when the seven hundred acre estate had been sold to horse dealer, Richard Tattersall, founder of Tattersall's Bloodstock Auctioneers at Newmarket. He bought the land in 1781 with money earned from his famous racehorse 'Highflyer' who won over 9,000 guineas in his short career and was never beaten. The sensational stallion spent a busy retirement at Ely, covering top class mares, who queued to mate with him at fifteen guineas a shot, a fee that rose to fifty guineas once he began to get results - three of his sons were Derby winners.

Tattersall built himself a new country house on the proceeds, and naturally called it Highflyer Hall. He filled his cellars with fine wine and 'some of the best port in England' for entertaining customers; the toast was always *'The Hammer and the Highflyer'*. One customer, a London silversmith, recorded that 'The house stood pleasantly on a rising ground surrounded by fine meadows: attached to it was a large enclosure, in which were upward of sixty high brood mares, with their progeny . .' The Prince Regent was the biggest spender at the Hall, often driving over from Newmarket during race week to inspect stock. Once he brought his friends, Charles Fox and Richard Sheridan, to see

Highflyer, a richly shaded bay horse with white left hind ankle, stands in front of Highflyer Hall, built by Richard Tattersall on the proceeds of his stud fees. Photograph courtesy of Tattersalls.

Highflyer, who was reputed to wear silver horseshoes made by a New Barns blacksmith. They all stayed to dinner, ' had a lively time' and slept at the thatched Lamb Inn.

The nature of Highflyer's retirement wore him out. Apparently no limit was put on the number of mares brought to him and he never refused to do his duty. He died on October 18th 1793 and was buried in the front garden. There was a day of national mourning. Ships and public houses were named after him, including The Highflyer on the corner of New Barns Road.

There might be a tidy end to the tale if ghostly, galloping hooves were heard thundering over cobbled roads towards The Highflyer pub on Friday nights, as drunks weave their way across to the fish and chip shop. But sadly this is not the case. Ghostly, galloping hooves do thunder over cobbled roads on Friday nights - but in quite a different part of the city. The ghostly hooves gallop along the much haunted college footpath, passing Firmary Lane, Canonry House, Priory House and the Porta - and eventually fading beside the former monastic stables, now converted into the King's School dining room. They are unlikely to belong to the gallant stallion.

9 A Sergeant-Major, a Militia Family, a Nurse and more Monks

A Sergeant-Major's ghost marches down Silver Street from the direction of the Porta on fine sunny afternoons, his scarlet jacket glinting with campaign medals. The straight-backed old soldier keeps to the left-hand pavement and turns left into Parade Lane towards his former home and the old parade ground where he once drilled volunteers on the site of the present cathedral car park. Scottish Sergeant-Major John Kyle, who lived in the end house nearest Silver Street, enlisted in 1793 and served with the Duke of Wellington in Belgium, as well as in Flanders, Holland, Hanover and the West Indies. In 1802, he became Sergeant-Major of the Cambridgeshire Militia, based at Ely.

Minister of War, Lord Castlereagh, had recently introduced a Bill to Parliament, enabling volunteer soldiers to train locally for 28 days a year, in an expansion of the regular army that would lead to the defeat of Napoleon at Waterloo in 1815. Each spring, raw country lads piled into Ely from outlying villages and farms for three weeks intensive training. There were no barracks for the volunteers, so they stayed with local families who were keen to earn cash by letting out spare rooms. Smart new uniforms soon transformed the gawky bumpkins into rollicking redcoats who spiced up the sluggish social scene - and as contemporary author Charles Dickens observed in his first book, *Pickwick Papers*: 'A good uniform must work its way with the women, sooner or later.'

Lieutenant Colonel Archer, an officer recruited from among the local gentry to knock the recruits into shape, noticed that 'human souvenirs' tended to appear soon after the new year. (He knew something of the matter. He bore a striking resemblance to King George IV, who was believed to have sown a few wild oats in his younger days as Prince Regent, partying with Richard Tattersall at Highflyer Farm.)

The permanent Militia staff lived in the Silver Street area. The adjutant's house stood on the site of Walpole Court and the armoury and stores were next door. The quartermaster lived in one of the four militia houses opposite the Prince Albert public house and the sergeants lived in Parade Lane, then called Smock Mill Alley. In 1869 a row of twelve terraced cottages were built for sergeants off Silver Street, in a cul-de-sac originally called The Barracks, but later renamed The Range. Each house had five rooms, an outhouse and a water closet.

Officers of the Cambridgeshire Militia taken during a period of training at Ely, 1859. They used the Lamb Hotel as Officers' Mess. Photograph courtesy of Chris Jakes and the Cambridge Collection.

In the late 1970s Annie (not her real name) moved to one of the cottages. She had lived there only a few weeks when she woke one summer morning as dawn was breaking, and saw a handsome, healthy-looking woman in her late thirties with lots of black hair, standing by the bed watching her. Annie thought she looked Irish, and marvelled at the dazzling whiteness of her apron. How did she manage to get it so clean? The woman was life-sized and seemed solid, but the insubstantial soldier who hovered behind her, was smaller and fainter. Behind them, three or four shadowy children peeped round the door. They were obviously ghosts as it was very early and the doors were locked. There was an atmosphere but not of coldness. 'Did you once live here?' asked Annie but there was no reply. The family lingered a moment and then were gone. She never saw them again though she lived in that house for ten years.

Four years later she told her new neighbour of the experience. Christine Pownell, a cathedral guide who had moved next door, was researching the history of The Range at Cambridge Library. In the census of 1881 she discovered that Sergeant Atkins and his wife Emma, from County Limerick, had lived in the house. They had eight children at the time - if she was about 35 - but later boy triplets arrived and received 'the usual bounty' of £3. Sadly the Atkins family lost their two year old daughter, Mary Maud, who drowned in a wash tub in the back yard. The wash house is outside, and very small. Mrs Atkins would have kept her tub in the yard and it must have been much in use, with eleven children to keep clean, as well as a supply of white aprons. The old lady who lived next door, used to see a man in a khaki uniform with red trimmings sitting in her garden.

A pale nurse walks down The Range from the former military hospital at the blind end of the cul-de-sac, holding a lamp to guide her footsteps. The hospital was built to accommodate thirty wounded soldiers, and used until the Militia left Ely in 1908, and then used again between 1915 and 1919 for casualties of the First World War. The nurse in her dark dress and white cap, seems to belong to this second period of the hospital's history. If she were not a ghost, she might find herself in need of first-aid. Every weekend she gets run over by boy-racers in Vauxhall Astras, who race along Silver Street in a deadly circuit of the city's one way system. Sergeant-Major Kyle would have known how to lick them into shape.

He retired from the army in 1852, just before the Crimean War, and liked sitting on the seat by the Market Square with his old mates, Sergeant Cuttria and Quartermaster Sergeant Knott. The three old-timers were at the railway station on June 26th, 1860, to watch the arrival of a rusty old cannon, captured from the Russians at the Battle of Sebastopol, and given to Ely by Queen Victoria. It was hauled up Forehill in the pouring rain by six white horses, and deposited on Palace Green where it sank in deep mud, until the Volunteers heaved it onto a stone base. Six months later Sergeant-Major Kyle died at 87 and was buried in St Mary's churchyard with the beloved red jacket, worn by his ghost, as his shroud, and a Scottish thistle carved on his tombstone.

Wounded servicemen and staff at the militia hospital in The Range, off Silver Street. In October 1915 the hospital was taken over by the Ely Red Cross Voluntary Aid Detachment for the care of fourteen patients. Photograph courtesy of Chris Jakes and the Cambridge Collection.

The Bishop's Palace was used as a military hospital during the Second World War and became a Sue Ryder Home in 1986. Ely's Bishops moved across the road to the former Deanery, where a legless monk appears in the 14th century monastic Great Hall. (No, he has not been quaffing town-beer - his legs walk below floor level in the 13th century undercroft.) The Sue Ryer nursing staff welcome voluntary help and are lucky enough to enjoy the assistance of a public spirited monk who likes to keep busy. One morning in 1990 an old man in a wheelchair went missing for a couple of hours. He was discovered dozing in the chapel, approached by three steep steps - which is why nobody looked in there sooner. He said a cheery monk had manoeuvred his chair down the steps.

10 The Bodysnatchers

On a murky November evening in 1996, retired nurse, Elsie (not her real name), encountered her second ghost in St Mary's graveyard, beside Oliver Cromwell House. Sixty years earlier she had watched an ethereal nun appear through the garden wall of her childhood home in Surrey, but the grimy young man with wispy hair who appeared from behind the holly tree by the belfry tower looked very solid indeed.

Elsie stopped beside the gate to wait for him. She was on her way to a meeting in the parish room, and as he was coming from that direction she thought it might have been cancelled. Light cast by the church porch lamp revealed a tall but stooped man in a dark jerkin, carrying a stick - or perhaps a spade. As he approached the yew tree to the right of the porch, he disappeared. Elsie searched for him around the tree and inside the porch, then carried on to her meeting, glancing back once or twice in case he should reappear. The graveyard is totally enclosed and there was nowhere he could have hidden. Elsie is a sensible woman. She knows exactly what she saw and told everyone at the meeting.

A local myth tells of a young woman who wanders sobbing around the graveyard at night, searching for her own corpse, stolen two centuries earlier by Ressurrectionists - or Body Snatchers, on the night following her funeral. Before 1852, it was illegal for surgeons to disect dead bodies to see how they worked, so they were obliged to buy them furtively on the black market, or practise their skills on cats, dogs and pigs - not ideal groundwork for performing surgery on live human beings. The most common operations were amputations of soldiers' and sailors' arms and legs after battles. The unwilling patients had to be tied down to stop them escaping, as the only anaesthetic was rum.

Yet as early as 1540, Henry VIII had allowed the Company of Barber Surgeons to take four criminal bodies a year from the gallows, for dissection at public lectures. (This famous killer of unwanted wives, was also a supporter of medical research to preserve life.) His daughter, Elizabeth, followed in his footsteps. She authorised the use of criminal corpses for dissection in the laboratory of Caius College Cambridge, along with the bodies of unknown strangers who died in the city. But as Anatomy gradually became accepted as a university subject, and a professorship established at Cambridge in 1707, supply still did not meet demand. The Anatomy act of 1832 allowed unclaimed bodies from the poor house to be used as well, but even that did not solve the problem.

Body Snatchers identified a gap in the market and filled it by delivering fresh bodies to hospitals with no questions asked. Forget the day job. The night job was a nice little earner with very few overheads. The only equipment needed was a spade and a few large baskets, though a pocketful of coins was also necessary for bribes. For very few coins, a poor old widow who found it difficult to make ends meet, would hang about the graveyard on funeral days and note the position of the latest arrival. Church workers were not so easily bribed, but one of Ely's sextons confessed on his death bed that he had turned a deaf ear to bumps in the night in exchange for a quick backhander. The biggest outlay was the cost of the carrier's cart - but it was cheap at the price. Quick delivery of a fresh body in good condition could earn the supplier as much as £1000 (in today's money), especially in winter when bodies kept better.

St Mary's churchyard was a particularly profitable hunting ground. The population explosion of the 19th century, along with the 1832 cholera epidemic, had made it very overcrowded. Bodies were buried in shallow graves and easy to dig up. Two or three men would enter the churchyard at dead of night and exhume a fresh corpse. They worked carefully with wooden spades, which made little noise and were unlikely to damage the valuable commodity; an unmarked corpse fetched more money. Bodies were wrapped in sheets, put into baskets, barrels or packing cases, and transported by stage coach or carrier's cart to the newly established teaching hospitals of Cambridge and London.

A night watchman was appointed, and those who could afford to pay, arranged for their relations to be buried inside walled enclosures surrounded by sharp railings or heavy tombstones. As usual, it was the poor who suffered. Their loved ones were often buried less than a foot deep and tended to leave the graveyard faster than they had arrived. Some families took turns to sleep on top of graves, as they believed that incomplete corpses could not rise on the day of judgement and would suffer eternal damnation.

In December 1830, chair-mender Charles Fowler and Irishman, Johnson Smith dug up the newly-buried body of Rebecca Shearman from St Mary's churchyard. They popped it into a wicker hamper and took it to the wagon office of Marsh & Swann, based at the Dolphin public house on the corner of Ely High Street by the Butter Market (now Peter Dominic's wine shop). Transportation was by carrier's cart to London: 'Every morning (Sundays excepted) at seven'. But Rebecca's corpse was not as fresh as it might have been, and the unpleasant smell coming from the hamper aroused the office clerk's suspicions. He called the constable who looked inside and discovered the gruesome contents.

Fowler and Smith were arrested, tried at the Isle of Ely Sessions in Wisbech on January 5, 1831, and given twelve months' hard labour at the House of Correction in Wisbech. If the 'hard labour' included some digging, it must have kept them in good shape for when they got out. It was a light sentence and perhaps gave some of their fellow inmates an idea for a profitable new career. As long as it was illegal to use human bodies for medical research there would be a market for dead bodies.

The case received lots of publicity and helped to change attitudes. People began to realise that if they wanted better medical care, a ready supply of corpses was necessary to improve surgical techniques, and public spirited citizens offered themselves for dissection after death. In the long run, this unsavoury profession helped improve our present quality of life. And by the time St Mary's graveyard closed for business in 1855, this particular line of work was becoming redundant.

This 1845 painting of the Horse Fair, held on St Mary's Green, shows St Mary's Church and the graveyard at a time when it was much frequented by Bodysnatchers. Photograph courtesy of Chris Jakes and the Cambridge Collection.

11 Waterside Wraiths

When Chris Wall drives along Broad Street in the direction of Waterside, she often passes an apparently solid woman with a narrow, pinched face and thin lips, walking along the pavement towards St Peter's Chapel. Her centrally-parted, dark brown hair is pulled tightly over her ears and tied behind. Perched on the back of her head is a poke bonnet with white tucks lining the brim and tied under the chin with two black ribbons. More white tucks at her throat are set off by a long sleeved, tight waisted, black jacket and a full length gathered skirt that reaches to her little, black buttoned boots. Dainty little hands are covered in black mesh gloves that reveal the pale skin beneath, and she clasps them in front of her and looks straight ahead. 'This woman is dressed for walking,' says Chris.

St Peter's Chapel of Ease, was built 1889 and paid for by Mrs Catherine Sparke, who might well have worn this style of clothing. Mrs Sparke wished to commemorate her late husband, Canon Edward Bowyer Sparke, with a useful building to help ease the cares of the riverside's teeming community. By the 19th century, terraces of Victorian houses were shooting up like mushrooms along Broad Street and the narrow lanes that led off it to the quay. The Cutter Inn was at the end of one and the Ship Inn at the end of another. The Queen's Head was on Quayside, the Black Swan stood opposite St Peters, and the Angel was just round the corner. All these public houses catered for the busy water trade and were frequented by sailors, dockers and prostitutes. The Canon's pious widow was eager to save souls and perhaps still patrols Broad Street seeking converts.

If the recently bereaved widow were to continue her 19th century walk beyond the new church, she would have come to some half-timbered, Tudor cottages that had seen better days and were sinking into picturesque, but neglected decay. The end cottage was known as Nell Gwynne's House, so it is possible that King Charles II's bawdy mistress stayed there too, on a subsequent 17th century visit to Ely with her royal protector. The cottage would have been a smart address then, and in any case, Nellie was under the king's protection. She was unlikely to have been in danger - but somebody else was.

In January 1994, a fireman, who occupied a flat opposite the timber merchant's showroom that replaced the cottages in 1933, heard a woman's voice calling 'Help! Help!' Thinking the voice came from the back of St Peter's Church, he ran across the road and searched along both sides, but found nothing. In March he heard the same voice calling again. 'Help! Help!' This time he replied in a loud voice 'I'll help you. I'll do what I can.' The voice stopped and was heard no more. When the young man told his colleagues at the fire station, they laughed and said he must have been drinking; but, although alcohol makes people sing out of tune, fall asleep in odd places or throw up on street corners, it seldom results in them hearing voices.

Broad Street was Ely's first thoroughfare, and probably still a cart track when the Normans arrived in the mid 11th century. The main highway was the River Great Ouse, and most goods arrived or left the city along it. Stone for building the cathedral came by river-barge. Massive oak trees were floated in from Bedfordshire to build the Octagon. Eels in their thousands were shipped out to London, as well as pike, bream and other fresh fish. At the time of the 1087 Domesday Survey, 52,000 eels were being sent court for the king and royal household. In the 15th century, channels were cut at right angles to the river to provide wharves where boats were moored, and open spaces known as hythes, were used for loading and unloading goods.

The open hythe in front of the Waterside Brewery, where the ice cream van parks in summer, was used for stacking barrels of beer for loading and transport along the river. During the 1970s and 80s, Barbara and Tim Eaton, lived in the converted brewery with their butch bulldog, Oscar, and used the adjacent, brick warehouse for storage. The three storey, L - shaped building had been a maltings, and the oast house used for drying hops occupied the foot of the L that lay away from the road. Its rotting, wooden tower was removed in the 1970s, and the square hole in the roof reroofed but not relined, so it is always colder in that part of the building. The first floor area below the tower was on a lower level than the front, and reached by a steep ramp. Oscar refused to put a single paw beyond the ramp. Elizabeth Goudge would have respected his judgement. 'My dogs have always known far more than I do', she wrote about the extra sense possessed by dogs, 'but then the power of animals are so exquisite that ours dwindle to nothing beside them.'

In 1986 the Eatons leased the barn to antique dealer, Graham Peters, who converted it for use as an antique complex. A workman sandblasting downstairs in the former oast house, heard footsteps above his head, on the lower first floor level, which Graham used as his workshop. His expensive tools were kept there, so the workman climbed the building's only staircase to investigate. The workshop was empty and the floor covered with undisturbed dust. A second workman owned a highly obedient labrador that refused to obey orders in that particular part of the barn, and would edge timidly around the wall to get past.

Since Waterside Antiques opened in November 1986, with sixty stalls on three floors, at least a dozen customers have commentated on the oppressive nature of the sunken first floor area, though none knew its history beforehand. A medium was invited to investigate but not told why. As soon as she entered the door, she sensed a hostile male presence - who could not possibly be Graham, a very friendly chap. As she approached the sensitive area, a heavy weight seemed to descend around her head and a splitting headache prevented her from staying long. When she moved away the pressure eased and the pain vanished. Graham decided to do a bit of experimenting and made a pair of ghost-divining rods from copper welding rods. Holding them parallel, but loosely in each hand, he set off slowly across the room. As he reached the corner, the rods swung violently across each other. He tried again in the ground floor area below, and the same thing happened again.

During the Second World War, that ground floor area was an emergency morgue for Ely's Royal Air Force Hospital, used in wartime as a special burns unit. Graham's ex-mother-in-law, Joan Griffin, remembers visiting wounded airmen of all nationalities in the hospital, when she was a young girl living nearby. Relatives of the burned airmen stayed at Joan's house when they visited. There were lots of deaths, and according to Joan, the bodies were laid out in the Waterside maltings until collected by relatives, or sent to the cemetery near Marshall's airport in Cambridge.

Graham Peters tries out his home-made divining rods.

12 Witchford's Wartime Secrets

In the spring of 1989, Bill Green of Peterborough and his wife visited Lancaster Way Business Park on the outskirts of Ely, to inspect the site of a proposed war memorial that would commemorate Bomber Command's 115 Squadron who flew from Witchford Aerodrome during the Second World War. Before returning home, they sat in their car for a few minutes beside the white farm gate that led to a field of young corn growing on the site of the former main runway. Suddenly Bill asked his wife: 'Can you see what I'm seeing?' She could. The corn was filled with misty, uniformed airmen, walking in twos and threes, looking up at the sky and waving. Above the continuous buzz of traffic noise from the adjacent bypass, the Greens heard the faint buzz of an aeroplane. The mist faded and a jet aircraft with its navigation lights on flew low over the cornfield.

Since the end of the war, there have been many sightings of ghost planes, usually flying low, sometimes seen to crash, but seldom accompanied by sound. The people

Corn grows beside the main runway of the former Witchford Aerodrome, now returned to farmland.

who report such incidents are often walking their dogs in remote countryside, sitting on moors looking for comets or hiking along coastal paths. Wartime airfields were usually sited in isolated places and in many cases, crash sites were airmen's final resting places. On 19th April 1944, two Lancaster bombers were shot down over Witchford after returning from a raid on Rouen. Not all the bodies were recovered.

Ely plumber, Barry Aldridge, read the story in a local library book, *Action Stations - East Anglian Airfields* by Michael J Bowyer, when he was planning a 'War Years' exhibition for Ely Museum, to commemorate the 50th anniversary of VE and VJ day in 1994. He decided to find out where the Lancasters crashed, and began by searching through old newspapers, but found nothing. Such incidents were not reported during wartime. His neighbour suggested that local farmer, Dick Freeman, might know as during the war he lived at the bottom of Coveney hill not far from the aerodrome - and was still there. When Barry knocked on the door and asked his question, Dick walked him back to the bottom of the driveway and pointed to a dip in the middle of the field straight ahead.

During the war, Dick would count the Lancasters out as they set off on bombing raids from nearby Witchford and Mepal Aerodromes, and then he would count some of them back again. On that April night, twenty seven Lancasters left from Witchford and eleven from Mepal. Later, when some returned, he heard them circling above his house waiting for permission to land. It was a familiar sound but there was an unfamiliar sound too - a foreign engine among the Lancasters.

A German Messerschmitt E4 10 had penetrated the circuit, attacked three aircraft at Mepal and dropped antipersonnel mines on the runway. The remaining aircraft had to find other places to land. One of the Lancasters crashed opposite Dick's house, in the middle of four small fields that were later merged into a single, large one. Farm workers used a tractor to remove part of an engine that lay on the surface, and the bottom half of an airman with his name, Jack Ferguson, stitched in the back of his trousers.

Fifty-one years later, Barry watched deep probe metal detectors test the dip in the field where the Lancaster disappeared. The search was a closely-guarded secret, but a hundred people and umpteen farmers stood watching. There were strong readings for three engines and a weak reading on the fourth. Grovemere Holdings provided men and machinery, and on August 19th, they started digging. Again the excavation was a secret so this time the audience numbered several hundred. It was VJ weekend and Barry noticed that the union flag on top of Ely Cathedral lined up with the excavation hole and the Witchford hanger, in a direct line with the wartime runway. The top soil was removed in layers, two feet of peat followed by clay for two days.

'On the first day', said Barry, 'they reached where the cockpit would have been, and Ray Woodbine came running across with something in his hand.' It was a small brass cross, its Christ figure slightly misshapen by heat. Barry flicked it with his finger and it came up bright gold. Later on, the diggers found a solid silver cigarette case with papers still inside, and part of a toilet seat lid with aluminium foil to fool radar, and some writing 'add chemical and stir vigorously.'

A war memorial was erected in memory of No. 115 Squadron, Bomber Command at the former Witchford Aerodrome, now Lancaster Way Businesss Park.

Barry showed the cross to a local jeweller who was intrigued by its bulkiness. 'He oiled the knob at the top and unwound the pin slightly, then it split. Inside was roll of paper that disintegrated as it was taken out. I still have the dust at home in a container.' An article about the excavation appeared in the 115 Squadron Association's magazine *Tiller*, and was seen by Canadian, Frank Kanarens, who had flown the aircraft between January and March in the year that it crashed. He sent Barry a photograph of himself and the rest of the crew. In the photo, they stand by the plane, below its starboard inner engine - the one that was partly removed after the crash and now lies on display in the Business Park's small museum. The following crew was killed.

Barry sent Frank a photograph of the cross, and then took it with him to a talk he gave at the Lincolnshire Bomber Command Association. 'Afterwards, a woman picked the cross up off the table, and then dropped it again, claiming it had burnt her fingers.' She suggested that Barry take it to a clairvoyant but he dismissed the idea. Four months later his wife, Sue, saw a notice in the *Ely Standard* advertising the visit of a medium to the Lamb Hotel the following week. It seemed too much of a coincidence to ignore, and she persuaded Barry to go with her and take the cross, though he was sure the medium would make up a story. 'If you don't tell her anything, how can she make it up?' asked Sue.

When it was their turn, they handed over the cross and the medium cupped it in her hands, closed her eyes, and said 'This cross has been in a horrendous fire!' It was obvious to the cynical Barry that the cross had been bent by heat and not impact, but her following words were more disturbing. She told the Aldridges that the cross had belonged to a Catholic woman from across the sea, who was widowed early and left to

Barry Aldridge holds the Canadian airman's cross, in the museum he helped to create at Lancaster Way Business Park's Grosvenor building. Photograph courtesy of the Ely Standard.

bring up two sons alone. She had given the cross to one of them when he joined the airforce, and he put it in his pocket because it was too heavy to wear.

'She said he was killed in a fire, not two miles from where we were sitting,' said Barry, 'and she added that the fire was so intense that it lit up the sky like daylight. The cross was in his pocket when he died, and his name began with M.' A few weeks later, Barry received a second letter from Frank Kanarens, who had found the surviving cousins of the mid-upper gunner, William James Macmillan from Garanoquie, Canada, the only Catholic on board. He had been given the cross by his mother.

When the 'War Years' exhibition was over, Barry set up a permanent display of wartime memorabilia in the foyer of the Business Park's Grosvenor building, where it runs itself during the week, but is manned on Sundays between May and September by Barry and volunteers from the RAF Association. The cross was placed in a display cabinet, and although laid down straight, it turned gradually until its bottom end pointed to a corner of the room, in a twenty minutes past the hour position.

'I didn't take much notice at first', said Barry, ' and just kept straightening it up. Then one Sunday afternoon a chap wanted to hold it, and I said "Well I have to unlock the cabinet anyway to straighten it up", and he said "Have you thought of checking it with a compass?" So I did and it was pointing to the crash site.' Barry tried stamping on the floor and jumping up and down to see if movement made the cross vibrate or pivot on its base, but the floor is concrete and the cabinet heavy. He tried positioning it the opposite way, but although it might take a week, or a month - and once it even took six months - the cross always finds it way back and ends up pointing towards the same corner.

Two years after the museum display opened, Chris and Peter Kerswell had spent a Sunday looking after it, and were about to lock up. As Chris came out of the Ladies at the rear of the building she heard a loud bang followed by a low rumbling sound. She thought Peter must be moving a display stand, but found him waiting for her by the exit. The office doors were locked and the toilets were empty. They called 'Is anyone there?' but nobody else was in the building. Chris says 'It was a very hot afternoon but my arms were covered with goose bumps and the fine hairs on them stood on end.'

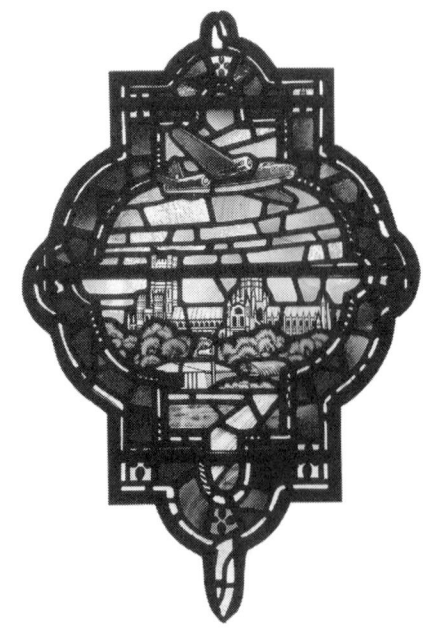

This stained glass window in Ely Cathedral depicts a Wellington bomber flying over the cathedral. It was designed by Liddell Armitage in remembrance of members of Bomber Command in East Anglia who lost their lives in the Second World War. Photograph courtesy of Ely Cathedral.

About the authors

Margaret Haynes and Vivienne Doughty met when they were both teaching in Littleport, a Cambridgeshire village on the fen edge. Both took early retirement, and developed second careers as Blue Badge Tourist Guides for Ely and East Anglia. Although neither were native to the area, both were fascinated by local history and legends, and came to love the stark, flat landscape and big skies. Margaret specialised in ghost tours while Vivienne concentrated on freelance writing. They decided to pool their resources and begin third careers as authors. Haunted Ely was published in 1996.

In the following years, Margaret discovered more information on existing ghosts and found some new ones. Vivienne moved to Berkshire and became a full-time writer. When their original publisher retired, they decided to begin fourth careers as publishers, calling themselves The Blue Hand Press. They start with a new, improved version of Haunted Ely. Unfortunately, neither author has ever encountered a ghost.

Vivienne Doughty and Margaret Haynes '. . . two middle-aged ladies who have put Ely's ghosts on the map.' (Cambridge Evening News) Photograph: courtesy of Cambridge Evening News

Bibliography

Books

Bevis, Trevor, *Historical Snippets from Old Ely* (Published by the author, 1995)

Blakeman, Pamela, *The Book of Ely* (Barracuda Book Limited, 1990)

Bradford, Anne and Roberts, Barrie, *Midland Ghosts and Hauntings* (Quercus, 1994)

Dorman, Bernard, *The Story of Ely and its Cathedral* (Black Horse, 1986)

Dowdy, Mac, *The Monastic Setting of Ely* (Ely Local History Publications Board, 1974)

Franklin, Alan, *Ely Cathedral - May I Show You Round?* (English Life Publications Ltd, 1984)

Gardiner, Rena, *The Story of Ely Cathedral* (Workshop Press, 1981)

Goudge, Elizabeth, *The Joy of the Snow - An Autobiography* (Hodder and Stoughton, 1974)

Hill, Christopher, *God's Englishman* (Penguin Books, 1970)

Holmes, Reg, *Ely Inns* (Ely Local History Publications Board, 1984)

Holmes, Reg & Rouse, Mike, *Ely Cathedral, City and Market Town* (The Ely Society, 1972)

Kingsley, Charles, *Hereward the Wake* (T. Nelson & Sons, Ltd)

Mason, H.J., *The Black Fens* (Providence Press, 1973)

Willett, Peter, *The Story of Tattersalls* (Stanley Paul 1987)

Booklets

Saint Etheldreda, Elizabeth Wilcocks (London - Catholic Truth Society, 1949)

Medieval Wall Paintings Silver Street Ely - A CHRONICLE, The Cambridgeshire Cottage Improvement Society Limited 1990

Oliver Cromwell's House, Pamela Blakeman, incorporating original material by Reg Holmes (The Ely Society)

Stained Glass - Ely Cathedral, The Pitkin Guide

Newspapers

Cambridge Evening News, Ely Standard, The Sunday Telegraph, The Times.